CW01671705

A RIDE ON THE ROAD TO EXCELLENCE

Three Men, Two Motorbikes, One Adventure Ride - Chronicles Of An Executive In His Never-So-Easy Journey Seeking Management Excellence

Dr. A. BALAMURUGAN

STARDOM BOOKS

STARDOM BOOKS

WORLDWIDE

www.StardomBooks.com

STARDOM BOOKS

A Division of Stardom Publishing

and infoYOGIS Technologies.

105-501 Silverside Road

Wilmington, DE 19809

FIRST EDITION JUNE 2019

Stardom Books

A Ride On The Road To Excellence/

Three Men, Two Motorbikes, One Adventure Ride - Chronicles Of An Executive In His Never-So-Easy Journey Seeking Management Excellence

Dr. A. BALAMURUGAN

p. 165
cm. 13.5 X 21.5

Category: BUSINESS & ECONOMICS/GROWTH

ISBN-13: 978-1-7332116-0-4

DEDICATION

This book is dedicated to all of you, readers. Within each of you, I believe, an exceptional success is just waiting to be brought out.

CONTENTS

FOREWORD

Humans always have the innate urge to desire for more in whatever sphere of activity they are involved in. It is this desire that drives individuals to achieve great feats in life. Whether it is climbing mount Everest, diving to the depths of ocean, soaring to the skies, performing musical feats, building monuments, setting up industries , setting up enterprises , setting up educational institutions etc.,

People who achieve such success have demonstrated how one can set targets for one's self and shown how through use of appropriate acquisition of knowledge, relentless hard work, things can be achieved in spite of limitations and hardships they encounter. Many of them have been inspired from what they have encountered in the Mother Nature around them and it is their ability to observe with great keenness and learn from what nature offers, that has enabled them to achieve their goals. Nature is indeed a great teacher and we can learn only when we observe with interest and keenness. We also realise that as individuals, we are only a very small component in the totality of cosmos.

As technology constantly evolves to provide newer and newer tools for people to deal with their requirements of personal and professional life, there is a huge impact of these technologies and their demand on ability of individual to adapt to these new avenues. This demand on adapting to the changes is also a source of severe stress for Individuals. If humanity in general has to achieve a high standard of stress free life, it is not sufficient for only a few or a small fraction of the community to achieve their goals. It is only when an increasingly larger number of people succeed in achieving their goals and that too achieving their goals without getting stressed in the process that the living on this planet can be a great experience for everybody.

In today's world of increasing demand on one 's ability to deliver results in leading and working with multi-disciplinary groups to meet the requirements of organisations, one is finding an ever increasing number of stressed individuals who are looking for effective ways to cope up with the situation.

While there are many training programmes, workshops, self-help books written about the matter of succeeding in one's endeavour and avoid being overly stressed or inability to cope with the situation this book, "A RIDE ON THE ROAD TO EXCELLENCE" provides a refreshingly new material.

Mr. Balamurugan has adopted a very interesting approach of bringing in the process of understanding the intricacies of various aspects of management through encountered experience in a series of travel activities. The experience gained through a set of activities involving riding on the mountains, SCUBA diving ,living in tents in a desert and interacting with strangers have all been effectively utilised to drive home the point. He has very effectively demonstrated the advantages of learning lessons through a practical experience route as it leaves a strong impression on the individual. Nature and its immense potential for a discerning individual to learn the intricate aspects appreciating one's role in life has been elegantly highlighted.

The book has been written in a very easy to read fluent style and I am sure the readers will find this book extremely useful.

Dr. A.S. Kiran Kumar
Former Chairman ISRO
Bengaluru

PREFACE

I found many managers, both in my professional and consultancy career, putting in extremely hard work and long hours at office or factory. And yet, they either feel they are not successful enough or their organizations feel they are not efficient enough. The stress due to either actual or perceived "non-performance" at office can be very damaging to a manager or to an executive, both at physical level and at psychological level.

While many organizations take sincere steps to give honest and professional feedback and train a manager to come out of those perceived or real shortcomings and skills, I see still an apprehension or yearning amongst managers regarding their managerial capability or skill levels. The best way to learn or sharpen a skill is through experience rather than just getting trained in class room alone.

I decided that I would write a book which can address some of these "Performance" related issues. What can be better than sharing what one has learnt in his own life through his experiences?

Having penned my thoughts about the workplace, now, my personal side!

Thanks to the support from my parents, right from very young age, I simply loved to travel to new places, especially, where not many people tread. And being amidst nature always made me content and happy. When I observed closely, I found there many things, we humans can learn from nature and its surrounding experiences.

This became a passion after a while, when I started driving out of town, for very long distances in my car and more so, riding my motorbike. In those journeys, I always found there were thrill, happiness and most importantly, lot of learning, if we care to observe. I somehow, always found time to balance my work with my passion for travel. Even when I grew in organizations to senior levels, I made sure that my work life balance was never affected.

There is nothing wrong in class room training or learning through various management books, which can form the base of the learning pyramid. But, if one experiences the management lessons in practical ways, then, I believe the lessons get imbibed into day to day habits much faster.

I found during my rides, when I really looked closely, I learnt many lessons which can be directly correlated to many management challenges of a manager.

When I started penning this book, though the content was clear, I was contemplating the style of presentation. Two books played a big influence on that decision.

One was "The Goal", a book by Eliyahu M. Goldratt and another "The Monk who sold his Ferrari" by Robin Sharma. Both the authors are in the list of top five of my favourite authors. And in both the books, the subject was explained in rather unique way. Instead of just making a reader to read through a book, he is taken on the journey of transformation through conversations, experiences and discussions.

In this age of boredom, where even 10 year old kids get bored easily, I decided to adopt similar "story telling" method of narration rather than simple advisory narration!

So here we are! Get ready for the ride of your life!! A motorbike ride, where there are management lessons learnt through the ride itself, from the people met on the way, from the good and through not so good experiences and through thrilling encounters.

And for the readers who have not yet started riding motorbikes, start by riding with the characters in this book. Experience the forests, mountains, waterfalls, oceans and more, as you go along!

Happy riding, readers! Cheers !!

ACKNOWLEDGEMENTS

This acknowledgement note would run to many pages, if I name each and every one of the persons, who played a big role in supporting me, encouraging and pushing me to write this book. But keeping readers' time in mind, will keep this note short ! My sincere apologies if I had left out any names inadvertently.

I ever remain grateful to my parents, both of whom were teachers. They imbibed me with the culture of sincerity, honesty and integrity. These qualities have stood by me throughout my career.

I am grateful to my In-laws who have put up with me with my adventurous life in the earlier years of my marriage (albeit little worriedly) and now, after probably having understood my love of travel and being with nature, are ever encouraging me to touch the impossible.

No words are enough to express my gratitude to my wife and son, both of whom tolerated my quite odd working hours while writing this book and also contributed with their opinions, through the draft stage.

My sincere thanks also go to the senior colleagues of various multinational organizations I worked with, for close to 30 years. I have learnt a lot from them, and those lessons stood by me by providing the spark for resolving all my professional challenges.

A word of gratitude for my friends from my motorbike riders' club, "Just for Rides", with whom I have spent innumerable days riding my motorbike in all types of terrains and those lessons have been brought into this book.

I also thank my friends and peers, who cheered me on to write this book. My special thanks goes to my friend, Sridhar for patiently going through draft and giving his suggestion.

When I wanted an artist to sketch my experiences, I came across Vishnu, a child artist from Bangalore. I thank that budding artist for creating right mood through his sketches for each chapter. My gratitude also goes to Vidhwan Dattatri of Bangalore, for converting sketches to suit print form.

Last but not the least, my gratitude also goes to publisher of this book, "Stardom Publishers", for their professional and expert support in bringing out this book.

WHAT IS IN IT FOR YOU?

This book is written for every executive who expresses or feels, there is stress in his job. He could be an executive, manager or owner of organization. The stress in the job mainly comes through various negative feedbacks about his performances, sometimes even about minor tasks, which makes him feel insecure and tense. These feedbacks could be from bosses, peers or from customers.

The feedbacks are normally given with good intention but most of us view and take these feedbacks personally. Instead of coming out of the situation and see the possible truth in that feedback and take counteractions, we tend to get emotional and allow ourselves to get stressed.

This book makes an attempt at giving a helping hand to such readers. I share a few tips on how to review such feedbacks and take corrective actions.

Each chapter addresses one or two such major issues faced by executives and through practical observations, suggest a few solutions to come out of situation. These issues could be Time management, Goal setting, Stress management, Risk taking, Innovation etc. During coaching and training assignments, I take a day or more for each of these subjects, but here the possible solutions are offered in condensed form.

This book is also written towards readers who happens to be, travel enthusiasts and motorbike riders, who, when they read the book, would be taken through a nostalgic journey through nature. I am sure, this book will take them to similar places they had travelled during their rides!

I have tried to use light conversational language, throughout the book, to make sure the readers are taken through the road trip of learning and travel, without much reading strain!

Few reference books or articles are listed in "Further Reading" section, at the end. These books throw more light about the subject I have dealt in each chapter.

Though this book is meant for discussing management skills, here and there, you will find that I touch upon certain environment issues too. As one of the characters says in the book, solutions to management issues are for making improvement; whereas environment issues pose a threat to our very existence on earth ! I hope the readers, do their bit, to stop or at least slow down environment degradation.

The reader has the option to start reading from Chapter 1 or randomly select and read any chapter. But I suggest readers to start reading from Page 1, to enjoy the journey seamlessly!!

PROLOGUE

It was a late evening. I was driving home after a client meeting in the city. The instrumental music inside the car was having a calming effect on me while I was wading through the traffic. Though I use public transport frequently, there are days when the numerous meetings with different clients compel me to take my car out.

My mobile rang. "Hey, got a minute for me?." It was my friend Arya and he seemed to be in some distress on the other end of the line.

"Oh yes go ahead, but since I am driving, make it quick, what is the matter?"

Arya replied, "Bala, what to say, I am in swirling water, in deep trouble, and in a confused state than ever before in my career."

I asked him what the matter was and he said he had his annual appraisal discussion and things were not rosy and he is on notice period to either pull up or move on. I told him to come over to my home the next day.

As an experienced professional, I find it little hard to accept, why Organizations always choose, most of the times, to give feedback to employees, only during appraisals? And, why an employee, cannot discuss with his reporting authorities on frequent basis, instead of waiting for appraisal day, for any feedbacks?

But being a Consultant, I see every challenge as an opportunity. And this may the time, I can help Arya to realize his true potential. Every human being is having tremendous talents and possibilities but unfortunately those are never realized to the full extent. Possibly, I can play a role, as a key to unlocking those possibilities with Arya.

I was planning to go on a road trip next week and I thought that may be right environment for Arya to explore possibilities of realizing his true potential.

1
PLANNING, PREPARATION AND UNLEASHING

Over a hot steaming cup of coffee at home the next day, my friend said with a furrowed face that in spite of his best efforts at office, his boss is not happy. "Can you be specific?" I asked.

"So much of feedback that, I am surprised myself" said Arya, "I was told that the feedback from my juniors and peers in the organization about me was less than satisfactory. And I am not a good leader and a big quantum jump is required in my communication skills."

"That is all?" I asked him.

"No Bala, I wish that was the end. Though I thought, I did put great efforts to achieve the goals, I was told, I don't take initiatives, I am not enthusiastic, and I am not a go getter... and the list is pretty endless", saying this he completed his sentence without finishing the list.

I nodded, and asked him, "So, what do you think? If you think you are good, why would you be receiving such feedbacks? Did you analyse whether they are incorrect or you have misunderstood your role?"

He just sighed and said, "I work for at least ten hours a day at the office, keep pushing my team, I put great efforts in every sphere of work, but I am at a loss where I am going wrong."

I asked him, "Are you happy at home? What does your wife think about family life?"

He said, "Oh, the less I talk about it, the better."

Then, Arya continued with a frown, "She says, she feels that she is married to a robot! She says I keep thinking about my work all the time, look stressed and hardly have dinner with her because I come home so late on most of the days. Neither my office folks are happy with me nor am I happy at home. So what do you think I should do?"

Knowing him for more than two decades since childhood, and from school days, I know that, since I was older to him by a couple of years, he takes the liberty to call me and take my help and suggestions whenever he has some challenges.

He is from a middle-class family and after completing his graduation, has come up in his career through hard work and moved up in the corporate ladder to reach a reasonably senior level position in an organization. Married, and father of a child, he is a genuine trier, but from what I understood from our discussion, it appeared he needs a break and think about the issue all over again. I thought, not everybody- his bosses, his subordinates, and his wife -could be wrong.

"Most certainly, Arya, we will discuss and find a way out," I said, thinking.

There was silence for a while. Then I said, "Let us do like this. Look, I am going on a motorbike road trip for a few days, starting this weekend, over mountains and other places. Since it is a holiday week, why not you join me? Our friend Jiva is also joining us on his bike."

In spite of all his troubles, Arya broke into a smile. "Oh, you are on your next road trip," he said and continued, "Oh my God, how come you are continuing to find time for your rides and other such things even now, in spite of your busy schedule in your profession?" he asked.

"Hey Arya, that is one of the things, you will find out if you join me on my trip," I said with a smile. "Moreover, the fresh mountain air will open up the closed doors of our minds and who knows, maybe we will discover a new thought process during our discussions during the journey. So, will you join us?"

That set him thinking. All three of us grew up from the same area during our childhood and know each other well. Jiva works for another organization, heading a bunch of sales guys and like me, has adventure running in his blood.

Arya was thinking deeply about joining this bike trip, as he grew up believing that adventures as such, are for crazy minds, who have lots of time on their hands.

I gave some time to him to think since he is one of those executives, who are proud to say that they are workaholics and have never taken holidays!

After thinking for a while, he said yes, but told me since this is his first road trip on a motorbike, he was a little apprehensive. I assured him that he is going to enjoy the journey and we will catch up the next day in a coffee shop along with my friend Jiva to plan for the trip.

"Was it so important that we meet again, to plan for this road trip?" Arya asked when we met the next day, in the coffee shop.

"Yes," I said, and continued, "The safe and successful road trip involves planning, as you will realize soon."

We discussed the route, tent, and accessories, first aid kit, servicing of motorbikes, spares to be carried, tool kit, ropes, shackles, torch, maps, Swiss army knife, mats, energy bars and even about downloading offline Google maps.

When Jiva and I were talking and planning about the trip, down to the smallest detail, Arya had a bemused look on his face, and sure seemed to be wondering what is this fuss is all about.

He said, "Sure you guys are planning well, but I never imagined it required so much of planning. I mean, are we going to use all this stuff during our trip?"

I replied to him, "Arya, this is the very first point of understanding in the office or on a road trip. Planning is the key to success. It needs possibly a brain storming session, with combined experience of knowledge, imagination and skills of the team, brought on to the table."

I added, "You would have heard or read about how Japanese teams work. They probably spend more time planning than executing, but then the execution would be perfect, without any major unexpected issues, and on time. Before starting any action or discussion, it is important to keep the goal, processes, and people in mind."

Arya asked, "Does this mean, that there are going to be no course corrections during the process?"

I said, "Yes, course corrections, if required, need to be done, but while starting our journey towards our goal, each member should know their role, course to be taken, and what to do in case of hurdles. We need to think of all possibilities and alternatives, and decide about the best possible actions in a given situation."

I added, "Planning does not mean, the discussions focus only on the goal! It also covers the journey towards that goal."

"You sound very similar to my boss at the office," Arya was smiling when he said this.

Jiva replied, "Maybe, the facts sounds the same, whoever speaks, right? The whole idea of a road trip is to understand the fact that, if we look around us carefully, we find solutions for our corporate leadership challenges everywhere, and we are going to explore and discuss these during this road trip."

I added, "Arya, during this trip, the ideas and solutions to your problems are not going to be taught by me. But the people we meet, Mother Nature, the situations we face, are all going to present possible answers and we will be discussing, as we ride along."

Arya said with a chuckle, "Oh thank God, it is not going to be one more classroom session of coaching!"

After about an hour of discussions and preparations, it was time to leave. I said, "Guys, top up the fuel tanks of your motorbikes and be ready for a very early start. We meet at the coffee shop at the junction at 4.00am on this Friday."

Knowing that Arya was never an early riser, I could sense little disappointment in his body language, regarding the early start! However, there was an agreement on the time and I told Jiva to help Arya to buy the stuff required for our trip. It was late night when we parted, bidding goodbye.

SUCCESS TIPS

1. Every single action should take you a step closer towards your goal.
2. Work backward from your goal and plot actions and resources required to meet the goal.
3. Be focused; there is no place for any activities which are not connected with your goal.
4. Every member must know how his role affects others in the team.
5. Every team member plays equal and important role, and no one is lesser than another person.

TO DO:

1. List down your goals for the next six months, one year and five years, both at office and at an individual level, at home.

2. Make sure the goals are SMART (Specific, Measurable, Attainable, Relevant and Time bound).

3. Split each goal into at least six smaller sub goals. For each smaller sub goals, have clear plan as to what would be the allocation of resources.

4. Do the same for personal / individual goals too. Goals to cover Wealth, Health, Spiritual and Family related targets.

5. Very importantly, while in pursuit of reaching the goal, give attention and enjoy the journey, i.e., the process. If you plan the process properly and enjoy the same, goals are achieved easily.

> Vision Without Action Is Day Dream.
> Action Without Vision Is Nightmare
> – *Japanese Proverb*

2
EMAIL PING PONG AND ELEPHANT LESSONS

There was a sharp chill in the early morning air. I wore my special biker jacket with protection for knees and elbows. And my helmet was worn over a woollen cap. A good set of gloves and shoes completed my riding attire. I stuffed all the necessary items in the side saddle bags and slung it across both sides of the back seat, buckled it up and was ready.

The clock was touching 4.00am when I reached the coffee shop, and Arya had just arrived there, hiring a taxi. His attire and preparation were similar to mine, except that there was a disappointment at starting so early and missing his morning sleep.

"Hey Bala, Good morning, couldn't we have started a little late?" Arya asked in a rather sleepy voice that clearly showed he was not enjoying the early morning cool weather! I laughed and said "You will know soon."

In a few minutes Jiva also arrived, and with a prayer in our minds, our bike trip started in right earnest.

I kept the lead role, while Jiva took over the rear. Arya was riding pillion on my motorbike. For a change, the city was free of any significant traffic, and we had an incredibly smooth ride out of the town.

The city looked beautiful in that quietness and with almost zero traffic, the roads appeared wider. And with the powerful headlamps beaming light on the road ahead of us, we quickly reached the highway and were breezing away.

We all had Bluetooth device attached to our ears but with the clear understanding that it must be used only cautiously and not for idle chatting, as it can be hazardous to converse when we are negotiating the roads in speeds over 120 Kmph.

After about half an hour or so, I pulled over my motorbike and asked Jiva as well to pull over, to find out if everything is okay and whether we can continue. It was still dark, and the morning twilight was at least an hour away. Arya was getting used to the long bike ride since it was his very first trip, but it appeared he too was enjoying the nice ride.

With not much traffic on highways, the road just zipped past us under our bikes and by the time sun showered us with His very first rays, we had already clocked close to 150 kms.

The Bluetooth rang. "Hey Bala" Arya was on the line. Though Arya was riding pillion with me, since we wore helmets and with gush of wind hitting us hard, our voices could be heard better by using Bluetooth for communicating.

Arya continued, "Have mercy man, this non-stop ride with chillness getting into my bones.. Oh, it is just unbearable!...Can we have a nice cup of coffee or something?" I said, okay and we pulled over near a small shop where fresh morning coffee was getting brewed.

Coffee indeed soothed us and made us warm. "I think, this is the first time, I am having coffee so far away from home at this time of the day!" said Arya sipping his coffee.

He continued, "Yes, now I know why you said we should leave early morning. We saved so much time. Once the clock hit 6.00am, the city starts crawling with so much of traffic, we would not have covered this much of distance."

I smiled and asked him, "What is the commodity we all have, on which we all have control on how to use it but not on its quantity?"

"Hmmmm...Is it not 'time'?" Arya replied.

"Yes," I said, "Not only during a trip but even on a normal office day back home, when you start your day very early, you would be ahead of everybody else, the whole day. Each one of us is blessed with the same 1440 minutes a day, but you always hear one person saying that he can do so many things, but few others say that there is no time."

Arya replied, "Yes, even I observed that, and unfortunately, I belong to the second category!!"

I asked him, "Arya, what is the first thing you do when you reach your office?"

Arya said, "Of course, I open my email inbox and finish all critical internal emails."

"And then," I nudged him further.

"I do clear all notifications in my social media sites, but only important ones, not all," Arya sheepishly agreed!

"Hmmm," I nodded and asked him, "How do you classify your inter-department emails as critical emails? Why not call up or meet up your peers and subordinates instead of mails?"

He said, "But email communication can be treated as a record about what was discussed, but that can't be done in personal discussion over the phone and can always be disputed or misrepresented later."

"By whom?" I asked,

"Okay. I do not dispute, normally! However, what if my colleague changes the commitment later?"

I said, "This is where the faith and confidence in our colleagues score over a period of time. Do you write an email at home to wife or kids to make sure that they do not go back on what was discussed with them!?"

Arya replied, "Of course, no."

I said, "If not, then you need to maintain the same culture and faith at work too. It is your extended family. You spend more hours when you are awake, at the office than at home. Have confidence and faith in your colleagues, and it will come back to you. In life, after all, what you give to others is what you get back!!"

Arya was listening, intently. I continued, "If at all you need, for important meetings, you can circulate minutes of the session but certainly no emails on day to day points, which can be resolved across the table or over an intercom call. I can assure you, Arya, you can convince, communicate and empathize better and have a higher chance of positive results when you discuss in person rather than depending on an inanimate email to do that job for you."

Arya was nodding. I added, "Email can transfer language but can never transfer your emotions and your views, as good as you can, in a person-to-person discussion. Moreover, the bonus is, when you discuss and sort out queries through phone or discussions, the time taken would be just a fraction, compared to the time spent on sending, reading, and replying to emails. You will end up saving quite a bit of productive hours."

"And add to that the time lost by people who are in CC or BCC." chipped in Jiva.

Arya said, "Oops, but I always thought, sending across emails was one of the most accepted activities in an office to avoid discussions."

"Remember, sending email does not always mean that your query or problem is resolved, many times, it is more like pushing the issue back to the sender, almost like a ping pong game." I replied.

Finally, Arya said, "Yeah, now I see, in my email chain, I mostly see numerous emails going to and fro, even for simple discussions, which could have been resolved in a single phone call or in a small five minute meeting, involving all. No wonder you used the word "Ping Pong" for the email battles we have at the office! Moreover, it is, such an abuse of productive time available to us- playing this ping pong."

Arya continued, "But you mean to say I should not email my customers or others who are not from my office?"

"No, not so" I said, "Remember, what I said just now is only for internal communications, but it would be still a good habit to speak to your customers to understand the points before you pop out your reply email. In that way, your reply would be more acceptable and appreciated."

SUCCESS TIPS

1. Never open internal emails first thing in the morning, unless at gunpoint!!
2. Use more of phone or personal discussions. Avoid internal mails as much as possible.
3. You need not to reply to every email, especially when you are in the copy.
4. Keep mails crisp, to the point and follow all email etiquette.
5. Have a day of "No internal mail" every week.
6. Do MBWA, Managing By Walking Around. It is healthy too!

By this time, we were done drinking our coffee.

I said, "Arya, this is just one perspective of how most of us spend time in non-value adding activities and then we end up saying, 'There is so much to do, but no time'. Imagine, if you can list down each and every such time guzzling activities, how much more productive your day could be!"

Arya was in deep thought and said, "I think this is going to be the first area of focus once I am back. I am going to be more visible, first, in front of my colleagues rather than in front of my laptop."

I said, "Okay let us move, and we have at least 150 kms more to travel today, and now we would be riding through thickly wooded Tiger sanctuary and then reach my friend's guest house on the edge of the forest. Are you game?"

Arya said, "I have never travelled in a motorbike through a forest, but as long as you guys are around, I have no issues."

As the Sun came up, the chill in the air gave way to pretty hot weather. As we rode along, frequent sips of water kept us hydrated. We reached the forest check post and entered our bike details in the register there.

We were frisked since carrying alcohol is banned. We were advised not to taunt or harm any wildlife anywhere inside the sanctuary when we pass through it. We said yes and moved on.

Since we were in the midst of the monsoon season, the forest was dressed up in all its glory. All around, one could see different shades of green, giving us a visual treat. The roads were reasonably well laid, and for a good and heavy motorbike that we were riding, the roads posed no issues, except for occasional speed breakers on the way, where we had to slow down a bit.

There were hardly any vehicles on the road, and the forest was silent except for the rumbling of our bikes and continuous buzzing of crickets. These insects could be found almost on every tree, and they keep breaking the silence of the forest by their choruses.

Arya seemed to be in a pretty pensive mood when he said "Bala, are you sure, this is the road we need to take? Look, not many motorists are around." I replied in affirmation, but Arya was still little apprehensive. "Is this the only road to reach your friend's farmhouse?" he asked.

"Yes, there is another road which can take us there, but it is circuitous and at least 70 km longer. However, why do you look worried?"

I noticed that he is a little afraid that we had taken riskier route through a jungle rather than normal, though, longer highway. Moreover, he being a city-bred person, wanted to avoid the risky forest route.

However, I was thoroughly enjoying sightings of smaller animals such as spotted deer, peacocks, wild boars, and birds of different sizes and colours which we rarely could see in a city. Unfortunately, quite a many bird species are becoming rare in the cities, thanks to our so-called development and the only things, other than countless human beings in town are cockroaches, rats, and cats!!

I could see Jiva was also enjoying the scenery and the animals around us with curiosity and happiness.

There were hundreds of spotted deer around, and they were not afraid of us and were grazing quite close to the road. However, the sighting of bigger wild animals such as Tiger and Elephant, I knew from my experience, is just a matter of luck.

"Thank God," Arya sighed from pillion, "There are no bigger animals around."

"True," I said, "It is always more fun to look for big wild animals rather sighting one. If you are lucky, you may see one in the next corner."

Oh boy, and we were lucky! As we were trying to negotiate a curve, we came across a speed breaker on the road where we had to slow down. And there he was, about 30 meters away, a massively built tusker, feeding on lush green vegetation, just next to the road!

While I slowed down to evaluate the situation and see how the big Elephant is reacting to our presence, Arya almost jumped out of pillion seat, out of sheer fear. "Oh my God, it is an Elephant, and he is huge!! Bala, it appears, trying to free my work life from stress, you have brought more stress in my holiday life!" he hissed.

As if it heard Arya, the bull Elephant decided that it is time for it to get on to our road from the greenery beside the road. It intently looked at us, standing right in the middle of the way. I knew that, if it decides to charge us, then if we are not prepared, we are in danger of being trampled.

I just turned the bike slowly, keeping ignition on at all times, to such a position, I could always ride away from it, if it charges. Took beautiful pictures of the tusker, on my camera. This opportunity was too good to miss as a photographer. I could see Jiva was also doing the same.

However, by then, Arya was already in the panic mode. He was almost ready to get down from the bike and ready to make a run of it, away from the Elephant! I whispered to him, to just sit tight and see how things unfold. After observing us for a minute, the Elephant decided that it is time for him to show who the boss is around here, trumpeted and charged at us.

From my experience, I knew that Elephants more often than not, false charge to make a point and move on to their more critical task of grazing! Thus, unless there is no choice, there was no point in running away from it. I just kept calm, of course, ready to ride away if required, and continued to watch its charge for a few seconds.

I could sense Arya, who was holding on to my waist, had almost squeezed it open out of sheer fear! When I saw his face in the rear-view mirror, I could see that blood had completely drained from his face. However, thankfully, the Elephant lost interest in us and trumpeting again, started going away from the road into the thick bushes beside the road, where we could see a few more Elephants grazing.

I waited for a few seconds and started moving on again. Arya was sitting on the bike in absolute silence waiting and praying for exiting the forest quickly. After riding for about 40 kms, coming out of the sanctuary zone, we stopped the bikes, near a stream.

Arya was completely drenched in sweat and was still speechless from his experience of facing a wild Elephant. Since the water was crystal clear, we decided to take a nice bath and freshened up by having some fruits, bread and some snacks we carried along.

Finally, Arya opened up. "Thanks, Bala. However, what would you have done if the Elephant continued charging towards us?"

I told him to enjoy the forest around us and told him there is enough time to discuss when we reach my friend's guest house later.

After that break, we continued our journey, as thick forests faded, farmlands and fields made an appearance all around us. I could hear my mobile ringing and I picked up the call. It was my friend, and he asked where we are, and after knowing the location, he informed us we are very close to his farm guest house.

Soon, we reached the guest house, and all of us checked in. It was a pretty large guest house with many rooms, and some of his other friends were staying there too.

The night falls very early in these areas, and we were sipping tea and munching biscuits, beside a campfire. The environment was enchanting with a lovely quiet forest and nearby farmlands. The evening chill was all around us, as we had a nice warm cup of tea, in the warmth of a campfire. With huge trees all around, the air was pollution free, and soon fireflies were starting to be visible.

Arya was thoroughly enjoying the evening. He said, "It is so invigorating and energetic even to sit and take some deep breaths over here. Being a city guy, I did not know, there exists a world such as this. No doubt, I travelled earlier, but everywhere we used to stay in the midst of noise and hustle of the cities. This is so peaceful and enjoyable and brings so much of freshness."

I was happy to see Arya enjoying himself. He was realizing that this is how nature intended us to be. Not in cities, where there are just colonies of humans, devoid of space for any other species and we have reached a situation where we need air purifiers to supply clean air to us.

The lavish living in multi-storied apartments and poor living in a slum, both are suffering from noise, water, air pollution. Nature has a way of not discriminating!

My friend is a plantation owner with acres of Areca nut and Plantain trees all around his guesthouse, and he lived a little away, in his own house. He had this guesthouse built very long time back, and let it out to his friends and acquaintances, who needed a place to rest during their journeys.

After a while, a hot and spicy dinner prepared at his home was brought to guests staying in his guesthouse. After having a sumptuous meal with other guests in the dining hall, we reached the cottages which were allotted to us and decided to sit outside and chat for a while.

"Now let me repeat my question, Bala," Arya said, "what you would have done if the Elephant continued its charge towards us? How you would have stopped its charge?"

I smiled and told him, if you think about it, not much! We cannot stop an Elephant easily from its charge, but please do remember that we were prepared, and most probably we would have escaped unhurt."

"But how was it possible for you to stay so calm?"

"Dear Arya, I think it is nothing different than what we face in the corporate world", I was sipping my green tea which I prepared after dinner. "Tell me something, when you are in office, do things go always in the way you want?!"

"Of course, no" said Arya.

I continued, "Even when you face an unexpected situation, do you always face benign situations or occasionally face situations which take you by surprise, storm and make you uncomfortable?"

After thinking for a while, Arya said, "Yes, there are occasions which are unexpected and make you little scary from a business or operations perspective."

"So, while the leader cannot always predict future situations, what he can do is, be prepared and be ready with alternate plans without panicking."

"So you were ready when the Elephant suddenly appeared?" teased Arya.

"Yes. Had you observed me, I kept the bike engine on, all the time watching the Elephant's body language, turned the bike around little so that I can ride away if so required, maintaining eye contact with the Elephant and more than anything else not panicking. Also, I had a flare with me, just in case."

I added, "Panic would have dimmed my thinking powers and slowed down my reaction time if there was a need for quick action. Knowing and studying about Elephants gives confidence, as is keeping the bike well maintained and making sure it will not misbehave during an emergency situation."

"Oh my God, all that was in my mind at that time was, how to run!"

"But dear friend, as in life and in business, you cannot run away from a difficult situation. For your information, in spite of its size, a bull Elephant, if you start running, will catch up with you in the blink of an eye."

"But all this trouble could have been avoided if we had that long road to this place."

"True. But we would have reached around three hours later, and we would have missed the nice sunset, campfire, and tea. By the way, when the going gets tough, the tough get going."

I explained, "A tough leader is the one, who is willing to plan for reaching success or his goal, in shortest possible way, taking care to plan for overcoming obstacles that might come on the way. The present competitive situation is such that you need to run faster and faster every day, just to be in the same place!"

Saying this, I bid goodnight to my friend, went into my cottage to prepare the bed.

Arya, instead of immediately going into his cottage, was

thinking over the day's events quietly.

SUCCESS TIPS

1. As a leader, you cannot always avoid an emergency.
2. Go through all possible emergencies that may arise and be prepared.
3. If and when an Emergency situation occurs, do not panic. As a leader, you need to inspire confidence.
4. Always have alternate and backup plans.
5. Lead from the front and protect your team.
6. Remain calm, and you will find solutions more efficiently.
7. Practice for possible emergencies, routinely.

To Do:

1. In your office, encourage people to talk to each other to find solutions. Discourage teams shooting off mails internally, for trivial issues.

2. Limit or reduce the time spent on social media at office (and even at home). It is a time killer. Treat social media as necessary tool to improve your knowledge, skills and visibility.

3. In your business or office situation, list down all possibilities, where things can go wrong.

4. Brainstorm and arrive at possible action plan for every one of those unfavorable and unexpected situations.

5. List down how your business can, positively or

otherwise, be affected by future technologies. Evaluate whether your organization is ready with a road map, to cope with such changes.

> The Bad News Is Time Flies, And Good News Is You're The Pilot
> – *Michael Astshuler*

3
OPPORTUNITIES GALORE!!

The wake-up alarm in the morning was nothing of the sort,that one wakes up to, back home. I was woken up by the calls of Deer and the chirping of birds of various kinds.

We were served piping hot tea at our cottages, which tasted delicious. Carrying a teacup, I came out of the building, and the whole environment was just out of a postcards. The morning weather was cold and the early morning mist spread out everywhere creating a grey wall, reducing visibility to less than 50 meters. The trees were trying to come out of their slumber too.

One could see different species of birds starting their day with energy and vigour. While some were proving the proverb "early bird gets the worm," some Woodpeckers were intent on making a hole in the tree with a "tut tut tut" sound, few Bee catchers were busy flying around catching a few bees as their morning breakfast.

One could also see a few Malabar Thrushes just content in sitting on the branches, creating their own symphony, singing away to glory.

"Good morning," says Arya who just walked in from his cottage, sipping his tea, and he too was enjoying this lovely morning.

"Good morning Arya. It looks like you had a good rest last night. Is it not?"

"Oh yes, believe me, had one of the best-undisturbed sleep after a long time. Maybe due to the tiredness of, all the riding, we did yesterday. However, this morning I am feeling refreshed."

He continued, "But Bala, when we have a place as beautiful as this, what are we doing in cities in the midst of pollution, thick population, morning rush hours, not so pleasant noises of vehicles, blaring horns and generally leading an unhealthy life?"

"Arya,that is the choice made by us, when we moved to big cities. Life always balances things out. You get a so-called better life, facilities, employment and money, which gets balanced by things you said. However, at least one should take time off once in a while to come off that artificial life and enjoy the real serenity of nature, to places such as this."

As Arya was thinking, I added, "In my opinion, a city is a place for earning money with many compromises in life but not for leading a healthy life. One may buy a good mattress there but not sleep, whereas here, whether one has a mattress or not, we are sure to get sound sleep!!"

Soon Jiva also joined us.

"So what is the plan for the day?" asked Arya.

I said, "After breakfast, we are riding about 250 kms to a mountain and stay overnight in our tents. And let us unleash the Chefs in us, since, we are going to cook our dinner tonight on top of a mountain."

"Oh, that sounds exciting!" said Arya.

"Good. Let's get ready, pack your things, and we will catch up in one hour, at the dining hall for breakfast" I said and went into my cottage.

When Arya came out of his cottage after a while, he found Jiva and me talking to a little elderly gentleman over another cup of Chai. We called him over to us. True to his reserved nature of avoiding talking to anybody unacquainted, he preferred to read a book rather than join in a conversation with an unknown person.

After a while, a sumptuous breakfast was spread out, and with outdoor life making us famished, we filled our plates with pretty large portions.

Wolfing down the breakfast, Arya asked, "Guys, you both were talking to a gentleman, who was that?"

"You missed out on something Arya," said Jiva, smiling and winking at me.

Now Arya was curious. "Missed out? Really? What did I miss out on?"

I intervened and said, "You missed out meeting the boss of one of the biggest group of industries in India." I named the company owned by him.

"Surprising! I did not expect such a person, to be here" said Arya.

Jiva continued, "Precisely, even we did not expect to see him here. We understood that he loves being with nature, and he takes a break once a while to spend some time over here in my friend's cottage. He was such a nice gentleman. He shared his story on how he built his empire, his thoughts and ideas for future."

I said, "Back in his headquarters, one need to fix an appointment, if he is in the country, at least a week before. That too, just to meet him for a minute, in his busy schedule. Here he was, talking to us, one on one, with all the time in the world, like a friend".

I added, "To share a secret, to top it all, Jiva almost closed a deal with him for selling his products to his company and will be having a meeting with him, after our trip!"

Arya was now a little crestfallen. "Guys, I have heard a lot about him but never seen him before, and now it looks like I missed out a great opportunity. However, he never looked like the owner of such a big business empire".

"That is another lesson learned, Arya," said Jiva, "Never be with yourself all the time. Use the opportunities of meeting and talking to strangers. Not only may you end up making some good friends, but possibly that may be the starting point to a good business relationship. And God knows, for all that matters, he may become your future employer!"

Jiva continued, "One of my top clients is the one, whom I met on the flight during my trip to Europe. In my experience, I can say, most of the business takes place, more because of personal rapport and good references, rather than only due to price, quality and other features of your product or service. While our books on Marketing Management can give good theory base, ultimately what matters is our street smartness in creating and converting those opportunities."

I can see Jiva was going full steam as a Sales guy!

I added, "Only a bad salesman will say that there is no market!" and continued, "don't judge the book by its cover and a man by his looks."

I further added, "This is an age of networking Arya, and as you know, people and companies pay money to get contact details and phone numbers and with economy opening up and our youngsters boldly becoming entrepreneurs, there is a lot to learn all around."

"Yes dude," said Arya, "opportunities are everywhere; only thing we need to do is, to keep our eyes and ears wide open. Is it not?"

After a good breakfast, we packed some grocery items required for preparing our night dinner. Buckled up the bags tightly to the bike, we were ready to leave. Met my friend who owned the guest house, and thanked him for his hospitality.

Arya asked him, "Look like you are well connected. Do you keep getting big guys regularly as your clients?"

My friend replied, "By God's grace, yes! Over a period of last few years, my place over here has become an attraction for many well-known individuals. Sometimes a few organizations conduct their annual sales meeting and other such meetings here. Maybe it is all due to the peaceful and pristine surroundings over here. Moreover, it is not very far away from your city too".

He added, "You may also consider bringing your team over here, for a weekend trip."

We bid him goodbye, and started our motorbikes and rode towards the mountains.

We rode very slowly, taking in the beauty of our surroundings. After a few minutes I asked, "Arya, you seem to be thinking of something!"

Arya said, "As your friend suggested, I was contemplating bringing my team over here for a weekend trip. Our team outing is overdue."

Jiva heard that since bikes were travelling very slowly and was smiling, "See Arya, even though Bala's friend spoke to you for just about a couple of minutes, he has created a client in you, for him."

We all smiled and rode on to our next destination.

SUCCESS TIPS

1. Take a break from work often and be with nature. You need that break, and you deserve it.
2. Life never gives exactly what you want. It provides opportunities and situations, and it is up to you, to convert them to get the result you want. Keep an eye open all the time. Better keep both eyes open!
3. Underestimate any person, at your own risk. Don't judge anybody by his attire, looks or language. Each person has an unpolished gem of a genius within him.
4. Do not hesitate to talk to strangers, and they may have solutions to your problems!
5. Hone your communication skills, both verbal and written.
6. Warren Buffet says, "The one easy way to become worth, at least, 50 % more than you are now, is to hone your communication skills". There is a big truth in what he said!!

TO DO:

1. Self-analyse, where you stand on your communication skills.

2. List down strong and weak points in both verbal and written communication skills and make a time bound plan to improve. Have you heard about Elevator pitch / Speech? If yes, practice it, and if no, learn it.

3. Practice good body language techniques. It is another valuable communication tool.

4. Never lose an opportunity to strike a conversation with a stranger, of course, without being intrusive! Talk to at least one person who is a complete stranger every week.

5. Create and be part of a good network of like-minded people or organizations.

6. List down various opportunities missed out by you and honestly analyse to find out why you missed it out. Most probably, you did not realize that was an opportunity!

> Most People Never Get Wealthy Simply Because They Are Not Trained To Recognize Opportunities Right In Front Of Them
>
> – *Robert Kiyosaki*

4
ENTREPRENEURSHIP SPIRIT IN NO MAN'S LAND

As we rode on, there was a chill in the air even after 10.30am. Of course, the roads were good, and we were maintaining a steady speed towards the mountain. Though I had warned both Arya and Jiva that Chai break would be at least a couple of hours away, I too yearned for a cup in that weather.

Not surprisingly, my Bluetooth buzzed!

“Hi, Bala,” voice of Arya crackled from pillion, “when do we break the journey for a Chai?”

“Shortly. I know a place where you get good Chai or Coffee”, I told him.

However, Arya continued, “This place is such a goddamn desolate place with nobody around for miles on end.”

I smiled and said, “Do you expect this mountain to be in the middle of a city?! Of course, the route to a mountain would be quite lonely!”

After riding for another 30 kms, finally, we could see, out of nowhere, a small shop, where we parked and eventually killed the engines. All three of us trooped in. All we could see was a small space built around a tree trunk, with few cupboards filled with coffee and tea powder, chocolates, biscuits, packets of chips, etc.

We found a pot of water on a stove, heated by a jungle wood. There was an old lady who was cleaning some stuff.

After freshening up, Arya asked, "Hey Old Lady, What the hell you are doing in this wilderness, in the middle of nowhere?"

The old lady chuckled, "I am preparing tea for you guys, and I live in the village, just a distance away from the road."

Arya could not stop continuing, "But you have a shop in this lonely place with nobody around, how do you make a living?"

She said "God has been kind to me. Tea for all of you?"

We said yes, and she went back to prepare tea for us. We picked up a couple of biscuit packets and started munching.

I asked Arya "What do you think? Is it a good decision for her to open a shop here?"

"I wonder..." Arya said.

Jiva pitched in "Bala, I think it is a smart move, because in the whole stretch of about 50 kms, this is the only shop, and sure enough, every person passing through this route will certainly stop in her shop. She has a 100 % success rate in getting clients."

I said "That is the point. I would say, this lady may come from a small hamlet but has fantastic business acumen. While everybody in her village is into farming, collecting jungle products, etc., she opened a shop where none existed, and now she has 100% clientele!"

Jiva continued, "Even though she priced the products little high, nobody is complaining since they are getting a break, cup of hot tea and little things such as biscuit packets which were not available for the whole stretch."

"Oh yes, I got it now," said Arya, "By running this tiny shop, she must be one of the richest people in her village."

"Yes, young men," the proud answer came from the old lady, who handed our tea to us, giving us a toothless smile.

And she continued, "Now, I do not depend on anybody. All I do is prepare hot coffee or tea, and I have customers from all across the country! I go once a week to a nearby town and bring the stuff required for my shop. I have been here for almost 30 years."

"Moreover, most of the customers I have are repeat customers or who come here by word of mouth. This keeps me engaged and makes me, a reasonably well off person in this village" As she was talking, a minibus rolled into stop near her shop with her new set of customers. She went to attend her new customers.

Arya said, "Thinking about this lady, she took the bold step of not following blindly what everyone else in her village did. And succeeded too!! I am not sure whether in my office, I would have allowed somebody to work or think in a different way than all others."

I said, "Important point here is, if anybody comes with an idea or a plan which is completely different than all others, the person need not be ridiculed. And always going with flow, need not be the best decision. While majority decision is to be respected, one need to encourage and accept differing points of views too."

Arya nodded, "Very true. I read somewhere only dead wood and dead fishes go with the flow!!"

After a picture photo session with her, we bid adieu to that entrepreneur and ignited engines again.

SUCCESS TIPS :

1. Encourage your team members to think out of the box.
2. It is dangerous to have a team, which say "Yes" to you, all the time!
3. Create a culture where teams learn to differ with dignity.
4. Keep adding differentiators to your product and services.
5. At personal level, keep developing/ updating a skill, which others do not have.

We reached the base of the mountain a little past noon, and as we progressed further, roads became narrower and with many hairpins bends. The air had a "mountainous" smell, and even though it was the middle of the day, there was a little chill in the air. We could see the peak which was quite far away covered in clouds and in an emerald carpet of greenery.

"Wow," said Arya, "this forest is unlike any other I have seen before, it looks greener, and these shrubs and trees are not seen anywhere else."

Jiva said, "Yes, the weather and the altitude over here create completely different types of trees, fruits, and shrubs which you will not see in the plains."

Though we enjoyed the scenery around us, we had to take extreme care in negotiating the sharp bends. We could never go beyond third gear, and we finally stopped somewhere close to the peak, near a viewpoint, for taking in the beautiful sight around us.

As far as our eyes can see, we saw forests down from there, and we also noticed couple of streams with gushing waters.

Arya pointed at those forests down below and said "Somewhere there, the old lady has a tea shop! I am still amazed by her business sense and acumen, even though she is not as well educated as all of us."

Jiva smiled and said, "It appears you are still in awe of that old lady."

"True, I understood our role models need not be only from corporate world, and they can be found in middle of nowhere too!!" quipped Arya.

After the customary pictures, we continued our journey. Slowly clouds enveloped all of us, and the weather became distinctly cold. We could sense the water droplets from the clouds hitting our faces, as we rode on. The visibility got reduced to a few meters, and slowly but steadily we moved on and within an hour found ourselves reaching open lands with lesser trees.

I said, "There we go. We have reached our stop for the day."

We unshackled our luggage bags. Arya was amazed by what he saw around us. "This is what I call, a room with a view, albeit an open room!"

From the peak, one could see all around, and clouds were way beneath us. It was like going back several centuries, with no human settlements to be seen anywhere. There were no man made stuff for kilometres around. This place is far away from any major towns and not many tourists come here. Thus the mountain remained unexploited by human presence, as of now.

After a while, we decided to pitch the tent for the day. Jiva had brought, just before our trip, a quick deploying type of tent, which the labels on the covers claimed, it would take just about a few seconds to open and pitch.

He said, "These are called, 'Pop up' camping tents. One tent should be good enough for all three of us. It is a brand new tent and let us understand how to deploy it."

Arya with his childlike innocence got very curious. "I have never stayed in the tent before. Let me try deploying it first."

However, in spite of quite a bit of pulling, stretching, yanking actions, the tent just refused to open. We could see Arya was getting quite desperate to open it and was working with all intensity to open it somehow. However, the tent remained adamant and tested the patience and skill of Arya.

"How come such a damn small thing is throwing such a tough challenge!?" said frustrated Arya while continuing his efforts.

Jiva pulled out his phone, and with available feeble mobile signals, browsed the video of the tent manufacturer, on how to deploy the tent. There was complete work instruction on how to open that 'Pop up' tent in that video tutorial.

He took the unopened tent from Arya and lo and behold, in just pulling one spring-loaded tie, in a particular angle, yes, of course, the tent did open out in just about a few seconds. We took out tent pegs and hammered them into the ground in all four corners, tied the ropes to them and our home for the day was ready!

There was room enough for three of us, and the tent was quite handy with many pockets inside, to keep the torch, mobiles, wallets, etc. and when the zip was opened up, it threw open couple of windows too. We removed our bags from the motorbike and arranged them inside the tent.

We were enjoying a little delayed packed lunch, which we brought along. The whole area was quiet, except for a gurgling noise of a stream nearby. The peak seems to attract some visitors once in a while, but we seemed to be the only team which pitched the tent over there. It appears that the whole real estate was for us, for that day.

We decided to spend a couple of hours exploring around. The beautiful stream nearby was flowing with enough water to have a nice and well deserved bath for all us and it was the only water source for us during our stay there. The water was too inviting for us to delay any further.

Arya was the last to enter the stream, and as he was exploring the water before bath, he said, "Good Heavens, the water is pretty cold, how on earth you guys are enjoying the bath?"

I said "All it takes is one plunge, and once you are inside the water, you will not feel the cold so much."

After much cajoling and encouraging words, Arya was in the water and was thoroughly enjoying the bath. "It is so different from a warm shower bath I have every day, at home. Somebody said to me, around 30 percent of youngsters in the city have never had a bath in the river. Proud to say I was one amongst them!"

Arya continued after a pause, "But unlike chlorinated waters that come in our showers, this water is clean of any chemicals."

None of us talked after that and we were quietly enjoying the bath in the river. We focussed on experiencing and enjoying the environment, the forest around us, carpet of leaves beneath our feet in the water and small fishes nibbling at our feet in the river. The bath refreshed us completely.

As we reached back to our tents, it was already evening, and we collected wood for the campfire, which would serve both for our safety and warmth. The campfire avoids unpleasant encounters with wild animals. We taught Arya how to start a campfire, starting from small twigs and leaves. The lighter we brought along, was put to use.

As fire caught on, we showed Arya how to slowly increase the size of the twigs reaching to the size of the wooden logs in a short while. The fire reached a steady level now and the warmth was very welcome. Arya tied the teapot above the campfire to boil water for our tea.

As we settled down for tea, there was an assortment of chirping noise from various birds, and the tea tasted fabulous, sitting amidst the tune of birds' chirping, in front of the tent and the ever welcoming warmth of the crackling campfire.

"Back home, around this time, I would be driving back home amongst that maddening traffic" said Arya and continued, "Sorry guys, but I am unable to stop comparing every situation back in our city."

Jiva said, "It is okay Arya, it is only but natural that we compare our city life with these environs, when we are in the lap of nature."

Saying this, Jiva stood up, went to the tea pot in which tea was already boiling. Picked up three glasses from our bags and served tea to all of us with some biscuits.

Arya said sipping his tea, "This is like a beautiful dream, which I want to enjoy when it lasts. Coming back to the opening of the 'pop up' tent, I never thought it to be so difficult and challenging. It was frustrating."

I said, " The frustration is, I suppose, is not just about a tent not opening, but rather, a feeling, can I say, an inferiority feeling that you are not able to finish the task, am I right?"

Arya replied, "Yeah, I guess so!"

I said, "Dear Arya, get this straight. We do get situations when simple things do not go our way. One way is to continue to struggle with that situation, and another way is coming out of the situation and rethinking about a solution."

Arya intervened, "You mean to say to stop trying to find a solution?"

"No" I replied, "Try to think of different kinds of innovative solutions. This can happen only by coming out of the situation and by viewing things from a different perspective."

"Such as", Arya chipped in smiling, "Google to find out the user manual rather than struggling forever to open the tent!"

"Exactly. One cannot and need not know, all that is to know, but one need to learn how to get that information or knowledge by looking around us. Moreover, in most of the cases, somewhere somebody would have already searched for it, and that information would be available on the internet."

There was a distant rumbling of thunder and clear signs of rains arriving shortly. Arya while finishing his tea said "So Bala, what is essential for me in work life is that, instead of learning each and everything that is there is to learn, which will be time-consuming, as a manager, I should understand skill set of each team member and use that skill to face a situation."

I said, "Each one of us is endowed with some skills and talents which team members would have learned through experience or by being exposed to a specific environment. However, unfortunately, many team leaders would not even bother to explore what talents their team members are endowed with. They focus on just giving directions, rather than observing the skill the team members possess, and using those skills, skilfully, towards a common cause or goal."

Jiva added, "And that means, giving up your ego and start respecting every one of the team members for their skills, knowledge, and then there you go, you will have a wonderfully performing team, each supporting the other towards the goal."

I said, "Guys, time for us to get ready and quickly prepare dinner before it starts raining."

We could see thunder claps between the clouds and they were approaching us fast. We spent a few minutes taking in the beauty of the approaching clouds on one side and a dim orange light welcoming the night on the horizon on the other side.

We pulled out the basic grocery from our luggage, required for preparing dinner. Arya went to the stream and brought water for drinking as well as for cooking. The campfire became our stove, and with three of us working together, lip-smacking dinner was ready in a jiffy. The Chefs within us, did not let us down! Just as we finished our dinner and cleaned up the plates, it started raining.

I warned, "Let us get inside the tent and thoroughly check for any insects before we zip up. As we were opening and closing the tent so many times, there are all the possibilities that unpleasant insects, including scorpions, might have invaded their way, into our room for warmth."

As we were checking the tent with the torchlight, Arya exclaimed, "Wow! The feeling of being in a tent when it rains. This is fairy tale stuff!!"

Indeed it was just like being on some other planet. The rain started slowly which quickly gathered momentum and became a torrent in a short time. The wind speed was reasonably high. However, the pegs holding the tent to the ground did their job well, and we were well secured.

The sound of rain beating down on canvas was like music to our ears. That lullaby combined with our tiredness, put us to sleep shortly.

SUCCESS TIPS

1. Keep developing new skills. Our education teaches basic stuff which provides a start, but the skills learned later, are the ones which takes us to a higher level, faster.
2. Update yourself continuously in an area where there are not many players, or in areas where future technology lies.
3. Use the internet effectively; make a point to learn something new every day.

4. Select team members with more technical knowledge than yourself. You cannot be, practically, a knowledge bank in the whole organization.

5. Start a small library at office or at home.

<u>TO DO</u>:

1. Run a check and find out whether you and your organization are "Future Worthy."

2. Technology is changing very rapidly in every front. Keep a tab on changes in your field of work.

3. Note down the gaps you are facing, to meet the skills / technologies of future.

4. Make focused effort to keep yourself updated and reduce those gaps.

5. Each of your team members will have a unique skill. Identify, nurture and use it.

Anyone Who Stops Learning Is Old. Whether At Twenty Or Eighty. Anyone Who Keeps Learning Stays Young

– *Henry Ford*

5
SLUSH, SWEAT AND SMALL LESSONS

There were still a couple of raindrops falling here and there, in the morning. When we came out of the tent, the rain had almost stopped, it was cold, and there was an orange glow all around. Sun was about to rise amidst the mountains. Our camp fire was completely doused by overnight rain!

Arya said "Oh my God, how many years has it been since I had seen the sunrise without being obstructed by buildings and other manmade structures?"

"Yes" Jiva said, "Indeed Sun is the energy tonic to the whole earth. No wonder our ancestors created 'Surya Namaskar' to enable body to take in the energy and Vitamin from Sun light."

Arya added, "We do not see Sun most of the times and work in air conditioned offices and pop in Vitamin D tablets!!"

I was smiling. "A perfect setting for a rejuvenating experience. However, here the weather can change very quickly."

As the Sun rose, the light brought bright colours of white, orange, blue tints to the sky, and to the clouds around and beneath the peak. With the cloud covered tall trees around us, the whole atmosphere and the experience were almost surreal.

Having heard that there was a small waterfall nearby in thick jungles, we decided to explore that. Our motorbikes had an excellent water wash in the overnight rain! Wiping away the water from the seats, we rode our motorbikes to look for the waterfall.

As we rode on, there was nobody around, and after a short while, we found a tiny bushy road leading away from the main road. In a corner, there was a small signboard indicating that the waterfall is about couple of kilometres from the main road.

We went along that small road and reached a point where the slope became steeper, and at one point, it was going down pretty steep even for a motorbike. We had a decision to make. We can park our motorbike there and walk down for about an hour, or risk a bit and reach down by riding our motorbikes.

After some thinking, I said that we are going to ride down. Yes, there is some risk involved, but it saves some time and more importantly, what the heck, it is after all for some adventure, we are all here! It required quite a bit of concentration to ensure we do not fall, while riding.

We reached a small plateau, where the last stretch of the road was even steeper. The loose pebbles made our ride down skiddier, but we rode down using all our motor biking skills.

Down there, there was nobody, and just as on the mountain top on the previous night, the whole waterfall was for us! The pool beneath the waterfalls had just enough depth to swim around. It was pristine water. Though his swimming skills are limited, I could see Arya jumping into the water and enjoying his swim, in the shallow cold water. While we were taking a bath, there was thunder at a distance.

"Is it going to rain?" asked Arya.

"Yes, as Bala said earlier, the passing clouds bring rain quite often here", said Jiva.

The ramming of water falling on our body in the waterfall had a soothing massaging effect on our body and all the tiredness of the previous day, if any, was washed away in that fresh water!

After the bath, there was no need for drying ourselves because it started raining! Since rain was due to passing clouds, we waited for a while for the rain to stop and once it stopped, we reached the place where we parked our bikes. We could see the whole path leading up from waterfalls to the road above, had become slushy.

When Jiva tried riding his bike up, it merely skidded down. Though the rain had stopped, the rain had loosened all the soil and pebbles creating a slushy surface.

Arya's voice was little muted. "Oh, my God! How on earth we are going to go up now? Are we stuck here due to this damn rain? Did we take an unnecessary risk?" The questions shot out of him quickly.

We could see disappointment and apprehension in his face. I told him, "Yes, we do have a challenge on hand now. It appears that we took a risk coming down the slope this steep. However, yes, thanks to that risk, we saw a wonderful waterfall. Moreover, we saved some time too by coming down, by motorbikes. Let's a find a way out now."

Jiva mounted his bike, started ignition and tried to ride up again, and the bike started promptly sliding down, in spite of Arya and me giving a push to the bike from behind.

"I think I will go up and look for getting some help from villagers" said Arya.

I told him, "The nearest village is about 3 kms from here, and instead of doing that, why not go up with the rope we brought along in our kit, to the top?" I mischievously made a cryptic remark.

I could see that Arya failed to get the point. "Yes, I remember we brought ropes along but what do you want to do now?"

"Simple, if we observe carefully, the steepest slope was the last 50 meters. I am sure beyond that, the road is still motorable. My idea is to tie all the ropes we three of us brought, into a single rope, tie one end to the front of motorbike and walk up the slope, loop it around once to the nearest tree and pull the bike" I said.

Arya was stunned. "Is it possible to pull up the motorbike in that way?"

Jiva said, "Yes, Arya, when you pull from there, we are going to use the bike engine power as well as push it from behind."

We tied all our ropes into a single rope, and with a doubtful expression, Arya tied one end of the rope to the bike and carrying the other end of the rope, he walked up the slope.

I pepped him up, "Hey Arya, you are a strong guy and all you need to do is, to make a loop around a strong tree and keep pulling one foot of rope at a time."

Soon Arya could be seen looping the rope around a big tree about 50 meters above and promptly started pulling the rope. As I started the bike and revved it forward, Jiva took position behind the bike, to give a push. I had to ride very carefully to avoid skidding since any over throttling, made the motorbike to skid over slush and topple.

So, with Jiva, giving a push from behind, and Arya pulling from the top, I was able to manoeuvre the bike, up the slope slowly but steadily.

A couple of times Arya failed to hold the rope tightly which made me fall along with the bike. Arya shouted from the top, "Sorry Bala, could not hold tight."

Thankfully, there was no rain, and though the route was very slushy and dotted with many loose pebbles, which made the task more difficult, we reached the top after about 10 minutes of strenuous effort.

Once we made it to the top, we could see, Arya sweating with his efforts to pull up the bike. I and Jiva were covered with slush. Though Arya was tired, we could see he had a look that reflected a sense of achievement on his face.

"Let us celebrate a little bit later" Jiva reminded, "There is one more bike down there, and we need to bring it up too."

Now with the experience of the first motorbike behind us, bringing up the second bike took less than 5 minutes.

"Wow, we made it. From the initial looks, I thought we are going to be stuck here for, at least another 4 hours till some local villagers are brought for help" said Arya.

I said, "Yes, even I was a little worried. However, see, this is where our preparations come to help us. More prepared we are, more easily we will be able to come out of difficult situations along the way. Moreover, the team efforts give a better and faster yield."

"Yeah Bala, thank God we brought ropes with each of us and no wonder you guys went into so much of depth during our preparatory discussions last week" said a beaming Arya.

We rode back to our tents atop the mountains, had a nice bath in the nearby stream to wash away all the slush, which had dried up and formed cakes all over our dress and bodies.

Since, frequent rains had put out our camp fire, we had to start our campfire once again, albeit on a small scale now.

We prepared excellent breakfast and a hot fresh cup of tea, and we all sat on the tent sheet spread across velvet-like grass around and were enjoying the breakfast and the tea. The sun was glowing again through the clouds.

"Tell me honestly Bala" said Arya, sipping his tea, "Did I get you guys angry when I could not hold on to the rope and made you fall on the slush couple of times?"

"No way Arya, each of us were performing a task which required coordinated work, and there was a possibility that any of us could fail in the given task. Jiva also erred a couple of times, to push at the right time and I also was unable to rev up the engine up just at the right time while you were pulling, a couple of times. These kinds of things happen in any situation whenever a team is at work."

Jiva said, "It is important that teams work with absolute faith on other members. Moreover, as we saw, in a team, no one person is a superior one. All play their roles. Each person is like a link in the chain, and no chain can be stronger than its weakest link. So our efforts go towards strengthening this weak link instead of blaming this weak link."

Arya added "It's like a buddy system in Army, where, when an important action is assigned, everybody supports each other with heart and soul."

I added "When we fell due to your mistakes, instead of feeling angry with you, we rather, could understand how difficult it must have been for you to hold the rope to pull us up, even though you are rather a strong chap."

Arya's eyes had some distant look, and he was quiet for some time. The chirping of morning birds seems to have brought him back to his senses.

Slowly he said, "Bala, now I understand why my team was upset with me. I was demanding results and lost my temper when they failed rather than understanding and analysing their failures and trying to support them to succeed. I did not empathize with their problems and just wanted results."

"Yes, the role of a leader is to facilitate a success not just demand success", I said, "Participate in success rather than supervising the success. True, it is important to succeed, but if you succeed at the cost of your team, the success will not be long-lasting, and it would be a one-time event. For consistent success, you need to be with your team and along with the team."

I was happy that with each passing day and each incident, Arya was seeing areas where our Business and Management acumen, can be fine-tuned. As we discussed earlier, the Gurus are all there around us, and only we need to keep an eye open to take in the wisdom.

After breakfast, we quickly packed up our tent and other stuff, neatly put them inside our saddle bags on both sides of motorbikes and were ready to leave. Jiva ensured that we left no trash and collected all garbage in a small bag which would be dumped into a dustbin later.

"I am impressed Jiva" said Arya, "You guys make sure that we clean even smallest trash, plastic, paper, etc."

Jiva said, "Where ever we go, we must take back not just good memories but also the trash we created there. The place must be looking the same, or even better, than how it was when we reached there."

Our thoughts went to a few pristine places in forests, monuments and nearby areas, where unfortunately, one can find mounds of empty plastic bottles, biscuit wrappers and other such trashes. We remembered reports where forest animals such as Deer and even Elephants succumbing by consuming plastic thrown around by visitors.

Sadly, very often, we assume that we have the right to create mess in every place we visit, in the name of freedom!!

As if on cue, Jiva added, "Freedom to visit a place also brings us the responsibility to keep that place clean."

"Impressive and very true" said Arya, "So, where do we go from here" asked Arya who was looking now really fresh and energetic after being a few days on the road. Though of course, we had briefed each other about the itinerary before the start of the road trip, Arya seems to be blissfully not aware or forgotten the same in the process of enjoying the journey!

I said, "The place where we go next can easily demolish one's high ego and bring him down right back to earth, and the place is called the Himalayas!"

Arya said, "My bucket list seems to be getting ticked off rather fast! Are we going to climb the great mountain?" The excitement was clearly visible on Arya's face.

Jiva said, "Obviously no, because climbing Himalayas is for experts and trained professionals, but we are going to ride to a small town right next to the big mountain range and stay for a day in a tent close to a river."

"That sounds no less exciting Jiva, since I have never seen a snow-capped mountain till now."

"All good things comes at a price, right? So, let's get ready for an eight-hour ride" I was laughing. However, Arya seemed to be primed up to the task.

Thus, we started the ride, through the mountains and winding roads, with thick forests all around and Sun playing hide and seek amongst the thick foliage.

SUCCESS TIPS

1. As a Leader, do not claim success was ONLY because of you. It is not so!
2. Anger not only reflects insecurity deep within you but also will never bring the best in your team.
3. Guide, participate and share, in the journey of success.
4. As a Leader, you should have a Vision. After all, you are on top, right!?
5. Your job is to make sure that the Vision is shared with the team, in a brain storming session, adding your ideas and thoughts on how to accomplish it.
6. Instead of criticizing your team's weakest link, put efforts and make it stronger.

TO DO:

1. Practice to maintain composure in difficult situations. Learning deep breathing is a good starting point.

2. Uncontrolled expression of anger does not show you as a strong person. If the weapon, "Anger" is used too often, it loses its sharpness!! List down the occasions you lost cool in the past one year and think whether you could have handled those situations in a calmer way.

3. Before you react to a failure of your peer or to a subordinate, think how and what you would have done better in his position / experience / knowledge.

4. Are you supervising and demanding success OR participating and enabling success? Think carefully and analyze which approach gave you more success.

5. Bosses can possibly win a battle, but only a Mentor / Leader can win a war. Which bracket you belong to?

> *Leaders become great, not because of their power. But because of their ability to Empower others.*
>
> - John Maxwell

6
WISDOM FROM A WAR MEMORIAL

The roads, though narrow, were well laid out. Thanks to pretty low temperature, we put on our jackets, skullcaps and leather gloves for protection from cold. Slowly, we could see small changes in the varieties of trees that make up these forests. From big and well-branched trees, the forest around was getting changed to coniferous forests, and after a few hours, as for as eyes could see, we were enveloped with huge conifers.

After about four hours of riding, one could see snow here and there, and as we rode along, soon everything surrounded by us was covered by snow. There was a carpet of white snow, everywhere, except on roads.

"This is stunning!" said Arya in the Bluetooth, "Amazing to see these beautiful snow covered trees and mountains except it is too damn cold, and I yearn for a hot cup of coffee!"

I said, "Just wait for another 30 minutes, we will stop at a very poignant place."

Shortly, from out of nowhere, we could see an arch in the road and a signboard indicating we have reached a war memorial. "Arya" I said, "Let us stop for a while here. This is Jaswant Garh War Memorial built in memory of war hero, Rifleman late Jaswant Singh Rawat, who sacrificed his life, to protect his men and his Motherland, during a war. There is also an Army outpost here."

All three of us parked our motorbikes and walked into the memorial. Though there were some people around, the place was tranquil. There was a big picture of Rifleman Jaswant in the centre with the photos of other war heroes around in a room.

I solemnly placed a bunch of flowers I picked up on the way, near the picture of that Great War hero, spent some quiet moments inside. There were descriptions about his bravery, selfless heroic acts and the ultimate sacrifice he made for the country.

After spending some quiet time, reading and seeing the details of other soldiers who were martyred there, we came out after a while. A small group of Army men were walking past us. While they were wearing uniform, of course, they also were wearing woollen skull caps and thick army jackets, to protect them from biting cold.

Arya was lost in his thoughts and finally said, "I am just thinking how hard it must be, for our soldiers, who are stationed here day and night. Here I am who is complaining of cold, just after riding for about 3 hours."

Jiva said, "Yes, Arya, one should never forget the great deeds and sacrifices made by our soldiers who take on elements and enemies day in and day out. Also, imagine them carrying the weight of weapons, rations, etc. and training and fighting for us, in such cold areas. We can never thank them enough."

I added, "At an altitude of around 14000 feet from sea level, the air is also thin, thus bringing down Oxygen levels in the atmosphere. This can make even simple act of walking, a strenuous activity!"

A soldier invited us for coffee. We were only too eager to accept that invitation! Led by him, we three entered a small building nearby, where we found quite a bit of warmth. There was a small kitchen inside that building and some hot snacks and piping hot coffee was getting ready for us.

We had a long chat with soldiers, who were only too happy to host us in such a remote area. We understood how they prepare, train in that snow-covered area and found the bonding between them something special. Almost all of them had left their near and dear ones in their far away villages and cities.

The way they hosted us for that one hour was unforgettable.

Arya was closely watching and listening to the soldiers. Finally, with drops of tears in the corners of his eyes, he said, "Guys, hats off to these brothers, who are ever smiling, ever protecting us. I read somewhere that we lost more men due to bad weather in these cold areas rather than to enemies. While facing and complaining about non-life-threatening challenges in our life every day, we should never forget the sacrifices of these brave soldiers."

Arya continued, "I don't think I will ever complain again, back in my hometown, regarding weather, rain, petty troubles in life, etc. after seeing our soldiers here, in these harsh conditions, who are sacrificing their lives, to protect us."

Jiva said, "Before we move, lets us buy some nice T-shirts and Woollen stuff from Army store here. I was told the stuff is excellent."

Yes, indeed the woollen stuff sold there was reasonably priced and of good quality. After finishing our shopping and thanking the soldiers, we were ready to move on.

SUCCESS TIPS :

1. Acknowledge sacrifices made and hard work put in by your team members and supporting staff, however small.
2. Celebrate successes with your team.
3. Do not sweat over small stuff!!
4. Stop complaining frequently. Be part of solution, not part of problem.
5. Remember, someone else is happy with less than what you have. Learn to balance aspirations and contentment.

"Arya" I said, when he was ready to climb the pillion, "Now we will be going through one of the most beautiful stretches of road, but don't move the body and shake the bike creating imbalance. Just sit tight and enjoy the journey."

We again bid adieu to the Army personnel and left. Slowly the road became even narrower, continued to be covered with snow, and in about one hour of the ride, we realized that we are riding on with a deep ravine with a fast flowing river, on our left side and a steep mountain on the right side.

The views were turning into a majestic one with snow-covered mountain peaks seen everywhere.

Jiva's voice cracked in Bluetooth, "Welcome to the Himalayas. While we enjoy the show put up by nature for us, let us be careful in riding, as one slip will take the bike at least 300 feet down!"

The river gushing deep below was in deep blue colour, and this snow-fed river appeared to be pretty deep too. It was flowing with enormous speed. The mountain on our right side was giving its own spectacle by rising to a massive height into the sky.

We stopped our bikes and got down at a viewing point. The whole area was silent with just sounds of gurgling river water flowing down below. Though the air was thin, there was crispness to it and we could see Sunlight reflecting off the peaks of the snow covered mountains. But the weather was unpredictable with sunlight, clouds and gusty winds taking turns every few minutes.

Arya said "This river and mountains make us look very tiny."

"Indeed. And, it is not that they are making us tiny, we are indeed tiny!" I said.

There were caravans of Army and border security vehicles moving around slowly and steadily in that road.

"How do these vehicles move around when the snow becomes heavier?" asked Arya.

Jiva replied "They do have different tires and also they also have a chain like attachment which is fixed to the tire, to get a better grip."

After a couple of hours of extremely careful riding, we reached our destination. There were rows of small tents in a vast expanse of coniferous trees and snow, in the middle of mountain range and a river was flowing right in front of our tents.

"This place looks fabulous, and what a place to stay!" said Arya, as we were checking into the tents.

"Hey Arya," asked Jiva, "Bala and I would like to take a bath in the cold river water. Are you going to join us or would you prefer a hot water bath in our tents?" Jiva loves to take to water at every first opportunity.

Arya said, he would join us, and we had to enter the cold water of the river slowly to allow the body to absorb the severe cold shock. Once we entered the pristine water, we had an enjoyable bath which just removed all the weariness of riding the whole day.

By the time we dried ourselves, changed clothes and came out of our tents, the evening had grown. There was a big open tent close to the river, which served as the dining area. It had 360 degrees visibility all around.

"Hey this is called, a room with a view, similar to where we stayed yesterday." said Arya as we were sipping hot tea just before an early dinner. The evening yellow glow of the sun was reflecting from mountain peaks way above us, and the birds in the Himalayas were in full cry in the setting sun.

Jiva said with a smile "Arya, some time back you were telling, how small we all look in front of this mountain. Why did you say like that?"

Arya replied "Of course, look around, the mountains around us are so huge, we are looking like nothing in front of it. We, our tents, all look minuscule speck of dust in front of this magnificent mountain."

I said, "I always used to say to all my friends, to visit the Himalayas at least once in their lifetime. Yes, as you said rightly, it just crushes the bloated egos of us by its sheer size. We realize that however big we are back home, whatever high position we may hold in our profession, in front of raw nature, we are indeed tiny and humbled. Just look at that helicopter that is coming our way at a distance."

I stopped talking and showed a speck at a distance, which indeed was a helicopter heading somewhere, and it looked so tiny in front of the mountains.

Arya said, "Bala, very true. I have learned my lesson for the day, by just looking around. This place taught me humbleness towards everybody. Our life itself seems to be a hired one, where we occupy this fantastic earth for a few years and move on, normally without much contribution to others or to the earth. Moreover, most of us think too much of ourselves, get into unnecessary arguments, then into bad moods. These mountains and rivers, immeasurably bigger than us and though are contributing much more than us, are quietly doing their jobs for millions of years."

Thus said, as his habit is, nowadays, Arya went silent. His eyes kept distantly looking at the mountains. We could make out that he is contemplating and organizing his thoughts in silence and we also were sucked into our similar thoughts with our eyes closed, opening once in a while to sink in the beauty of Himalayas.

We realized that nature is our ultimate Guru, if only we learn how to listen to what it is saying. No wonder, this place is a preferred abode for some great past Gurus and the people on the spiritual path. Even some rich Hollywood stars find this quiet place giving solace to their disturbed minds. Silence can be a great eye-opener too.

Finally, I said, "Yes Arya, as we grow in any organization, we start thinking that we know all and let our ego not to accept opinions, feedbacks, and criticisms from our peers or junior colleagues. The team can be won more by spreading knowledge and accepting ignorance rather than bulldozing and shouting at them, thereby laying bare our limitations. Humbleness and acceptance can be a sharper tool for success than arrogance."

"I realize an organization can have world-class facilities, products, systems, and processes but if the leader does not realize how to engage the team, it all goes waste. I read that majority of employees leave organization not because of organization, its policies, etc., but mainly due to the arrogant attitude of its leaders!" said Arya

Dinner was served with hot tea, and I was served with my favourite green tea! We simply relished sumptuous dinner served with the accompanying musical score of a river flowing next to us.

"My God, this symphony of river is so sweet! While I am not against music and parties in the cities, I wish our friends, especially youngsters, back in our town also experience the dinner with the music of nature, at least once a while. Our children in the cities deserve this treat." said Arya.

We retired for the night, feeling fresh physically. I was also happy for Arya who seems to have broken some glass ceilings in his mind today, thanks to the learning from Nature.

And as I looked out of the tent, I could see bright moonlight bouncing off the white peaks of the mountain, casting an aura of magical cool white light all around, creating a heaven on our earth.

SUCCESS TIPS :

1. Spend some quality time, quietly in nature. Use the time to introspect.
2. Better decisions are taken when your mind is relaxed rather than being under pressure all the time.
3. There is a fine line between confidence and arrogance. Effective leaders always keep a watch, not to cross it.
4. You may not agree to a point, but you cannot ignore a point.
5. Any fool can be arrogant, but it takes strength to be humble.

<u>TO DO</u> :

1. Do not claim you are a workaholic. Your mind and body need a break to perform better. So take a break.

When did you last take your team on an outing?

2. Decide who is smarter. You or your "smart" mobile phone?! Be away from emails, social media, and your phone for at least some time, every day. The world will not fall apart!

3. Learn how to face criticism and give critical feedback. Practice "Sandwich" feedback method.

4. How much time you allow others to talk in a meeting? As a leader, listen more in any meeting. You may love your own voice, but don't covert meeting room into lecture hall!

5. Are all your ideas accepted by your team without discussion, in a meeting? Don't be too proud! You are in dangerous turf!! Either all your team members are "Yes men" or they are afraid to give their opinion. Time to change the situation.

> The trouble with most of us is, that we would rather be ruined by praise rather saved by criticism
>
> – *Norman Vincent Peale*

7
RIVER RAFTING AND RISK TAKING

We had never seen such dawn in our lives. There was mist all around and high above the clouds, a golden yellow light reflected from the early morning sun falling on snow covered mountains somewhere up over there. The light bouncing off from the snow covered peaks seen for the third time in last

12 hours, but with each time with a different hue of colours!

As we freshened up and were having breakfast, I asked, "Do you know swimming Arya?"

I could sense that Arya was feeling something nasty or naughty is coming up. Jiva was smiling.

Arya said, "Guys, you know by now that I know a little swimming but nothing to boast about."

I said, "We all took bath in a small stream today. How about meeting and greeting his big brother, a fast flowing big river?"

"To take a bath on its banks? "Arya asked with genuine innocence!

Now Jiva was laughing, and he said, "No Arya, we are going for river rafting, and we are going to be in the middle of the river, in an inflatable raft and going to get all wet."

We could see that Arya's enthusiasm has given way to terror. "What do you mean by being in the middle of a big river and getting wet?! It looks like you guys are either playing pranks or taking my life for granted."

He continued, sheepishly, "I must confess, our encounter with wild Elephant, is still giving me nightmares and you guys want to add another chapter to my book of nightmares."

I could understand that it quite normal for any person to have nightmares after having such a close encounter with a wild Elephant! It appeared that Arya is no different.

I assured, "Arya, of course, we will not put your life in danger. All we can assure you is that you will have one hell of a time over there."

"Okay, let me reach there and look for myself" said Arya, in a resigned voice.

With one last look at the beautiful mountains, we started our ride towards our next destination. We rode on, almost nonstop and in silence, grasping the gorgeous views, riding steadily yet cautiously.

We stopped our bikes to take pictures with herds of Yaks being herded by local herdsmen. They looked completely different creatures compared to our city-bred cows, but the herdsmen informed that they belonged to same species, and they look different because of the thick coat of hair and solid layer of fat under their skin, to protect themselves from the freezing temperatures.

Yak's ears were neatly punched with their identity number and the herdsmen offered us to give Yak milk if we wait for another 15 minutes, but we said no thanks and moved on.

The roads went sloping down as we rode on, and though the chillness remained, slowly the snow disappeared. The roads were narrow but in good condition. We had to pull over to the sides a couple of times, to allow big army trucks to pass by. However, we had to be extremely careful since there were deep ravines just beyond the edge of the road.

After riding for about 5 hours, we reached our destination of the day, near a river again. While on the previous night, we stayed near a smaller river, this one was pretty huge with water gushing past us. We stopped our bikes and Jiva went around scouting for a nice place to pitch our tent near the banks of the river.

"Bala" said Arya, "Is this where we are going to start our river rafting? The river looks pretty deep, and the flow of water is also pretty fast."

Though I could see the excitement in his voice, there was also a hint of fear in his body language.

We could see Jiva approaching us after his survey.

He said, "Dear Arya, rivers change their faces very fast, this stretch of about 10 kms gives us a sample of how the river can change their faces. It is deep in some places, it is shallow in another, it is slowly moving in some places, fast flowing in another and it also has rapids and small falls of about four feet height, over and through which, we are going to ride our inflatable boats."

I added, "I would rate this rafting as between level 3 and 4."

"What, we are going to flow in the river over rapids and small waterfalls?! That is the craziest thing I heard ever" said Arya.

He looked at me, "And you are telling me that for these rapids, there are ratings too! However, it is amazing, how you guys ever managed to learn about all this stuff!"

"We should never end our life as one trick pony, right?" Saying this, I smiled and kept quiet. We wanted him to experience rather than explaining the experience.

We pitched the tent we carried on our motorbikes, on the banks of the river, quickly, having learned lessons a few days back. The sands on the banks of the river looked pristine white, and on one side there was mountain slope and on the other side, the blue river flowing past us.

We prepared lunch with the stuff we brought along with us. Jiva prepared fire using the wooden branches found nearby, and we helped each other to prepare lunch in about 30 minutes. We spread a cloth sheet on river sand, spread out the dishes and realized that we were pretty hungry.

We finished our lunch, cleaned the dishes in the river and relaxed a bit taking in the environment and the sounds nearby.

"Is it true" asked Arya, "the sound of flowing water has a soothing effect on our brain?"

Indeed, we all felt relaxed and Jiva said, "Yes, the sound of flowing water does have a calming effect on us, and that is why in our city, one can see there are shops in big malls selling small pump operated artificial 'waterfalls', which create beautiful sounds of the natural water flowing, in a room."

Through the afternoon silence, we could hear an engine revving, and we could see a small jeep coming towards us. Jiva said, "I called the rafting guys who are, as you can see, bringing the inflatable along with them."

Yes, indeed we could see a big blue inflatable boat tied to the jeep, on its top. The guys in the vehicle waved at us and reached our campsite.

One of them came forward and introduced himself as Pradip, leader of the crew. After mutual introductions, each one of us was given a life jacket, irrespective of whether we knew swimming or not, and the experts gave us instructions. There were four of them, and they seemed to know exactly what needs to be done.

Pradip said, "Guys, enjoy the next one hour of rafting. Our team has experience of taking our guests for white water rafting, hundreds of times. During rafting, we will be following the water, as it flows, in all types of terrains. And even if you fall off the inflatable, do not worry, you can never sink since you are wearing life jackets, and anyway, we will always be just seconds away, to pull you in. However, never panic."

These words itself, we can see, caused panic for Arya! The gushing waters, especially if you are not confident with water, can cause uneasiness. But we wanted Arya to undergo that trial by fire, to come out of such fears.

They provided a small waterproof bag to each one of us so that we can keep our camera and other stuff inside, away from water, safely. And each one of us was given a paddle too.

Soon the inflatable was unloaded from the jeep on to the river, and all seven of us climbed on to that. The boat slowly started moving in the water, and our tents were moving away from us. While Pradip sat in the back, three of us sat on each side of the boat and starting paddling.

"How deep is the river here?" Arya asked looking into the clear deep blue water.

Pradip said, "Arya, it is about seventy feet deep over here."

Knowing that Arya does not swim well, his reaction was expected! "Oh, my God, seventy feet depth?" There were signs of worry on his face.

Pradip said, "If I were you, more than depth, I would worry about the swirls and rapids more. Moreover, depth does not matter, because you are wearing a life jacket."

The view around us was getting prettier with small vertical rock faces on both sides of the boat, as we were paddling past in the river. Since it was downstream, the paddling was more for directing the raft rather than pushing it forward. We could sense that the speed of the boat has increased.

I asked Pradip, "Can I get into the water?"

Even before Pradip could answer, Arya said, "Bala, it's impossible, why do you want to jump out of the boat?"

But Pradeep nodded. I smiled, having already done it a few times before and jumped into the water from the raft. The water was, of course, cold, but thanks to the life jacket, I started floating along with the boat.

The experience was thrilling, and soon Jiva too joined. Shortly later, we heard roaring noises of water gushing down, and Pradip said, "Guys, come back into the boat, we are approaching rapids." Soon, we were pulled into the boat, and the boat was moving quite fast now.

"Oh, I can see water falling down a few feet down, just ahead of us" said the excited voice of Arya. Pradip said, "I would not call it waterfalls, but just river flowing down suddenly by about four to five feet. Just relax when we go down the rapids through the slope, and even if you fall down, you would be floating and we will get you back on to the boat"

We could see Arya holding on to the handles in the boat tightly. Soon the boat tossed and jumped around when it came down, along with flowing water by about 5 feet and there was water splashing all around and even inside the boat. We stopped paddling since it was of no use now. The boat swirled, turned around rapidly as it flowed down at ferocious speed and almost capsized.

As expected, we were all drenched, and we all let out a cry of joy, fear, and excitement based on our individual choice! After a couple of more such rapids, the river, though deep, was slowing down.

"This is phenomenal" a completely drenched Arya shouted. "Never done something as crazy as this, in my entire life!"

I jumped into the water again with Jiva, and Arya asked "Pradip, can I also get into the water, but my swimming skills are rather limited?"

Pradip was more than eager to accommodate. "As long as you are wearing a life jacket and supervised by us, why not?"

Hearing this, an eager but little edgy Arya finally jumped from a boat into flowing water. By instinct, he started struggling and thrashing around in the water as he jumped, but I held his hand and calmed him down saying nothing has happened, and he is indeed alive! He soon learned how to float in the water and he started thoroughly enjoying the same.

We could see the river carrying several things past us, such as wood, leaves and even a snake was seen swimming past us! Soon we floated past underneath a bridge too. Curious onlookers waved at us from the bridge, to whom we waved back.

After spending some more time in the water, Pradip called us back into the raft. We were all very wet but thoroughly enjoyed the experience. Slowly the raft was guided to the shore, and we could see the jeep waiting for us.

We climbed the jeep, and the boat was again tied to the top of the vehicle. As we travelled back to our tents about 10 kms away, thanks to our wet clothes, we were feeling pretty cold. However, after a short ride, we reached our campsite.

One of the rafting crew members had already prepared hot tea for us in our campfire. We changed to dry clothes and after drying ourselves, came out for a good cup of hot tea. Pradip and team were paid for their services, and they bid adieu from us. We requested them to bring some lovely local delicacies for our dinner, after a couple of hours, which they agreed to.

It was time to enjoy well-deserved tea break in front of the campfire, bringing some warmth to us.

"That was one hell of an experience" said Arya.

Jiva was smiling broadly now. "And you were accusing us in the morning that we are putting your life on risk!!"

Arya said, "To be honest, when we got into boat and river, indeed I thought you guys are putting me into a life-threatening situation. However, I must say that when I jumped in, I had an unforgettable life experience."

Tea was excellent, and Jiva poured another round of tea into our cups.

Arya continued, "Bala, I was thinking, if out of worry or fear, had I not come with you guys, I would have missed a great experience. Is it not? There were many reasons for me to decide not to experience this fantastic adventure."

Arya thought for a while and added, "I don't know swimming, the river was deep and fast flowing, it is risky if not outright dangerous, I was with some new team of rafters whom I had never met before, etc. and God damn it, I saw a snake too floating on the water ! However, I am glad still I made up mind to explore the experience."

"Arya, I am also delighted you decided to get drenched! What you did was quite natural. A human being, by nature, is programmed to try something new, every day, not satisfied with the status quo. Also, when you attempt and try to do something which is not everyday stuff, you will see your confidence in yourself and your team also goes up."

I continued, "Yes, one needs to take care of safety aspects, which we did, but one must yearn to keep experimenting with something new and what others may call crazy. At the worst, we may fail in that attempt, which anyway may happen, even if you do not attempt!"

"It appears that you guys have selected each day's adventure, to teach me a lesson to take back to my office!" said Arya.

Jiva laughed, "No, not exactly, but we are just seeing and analysing each day's experience in the context of our work and life. We understand how beautiful nature is and experience the intricate interactions, we all have with Her. It reveals many subtle management lessons, if we care to observe closely, right?"

Arya said, "True, isn't Bruce Lee who said, 'Life itself is your teacher, and you are in constant state of learning?'"

He continued, "Yes, of course, and today's experience certainly did teach me how not be content with what you are doing, how to set the bar higher, how to take calculated risk, how to encourage my team to keep looking out for different methods for reaching higher level, instead of working like a robot every day."

"Wow!" said Jiva, "You seem to be taking multiple notes out of single experience!"

I added, "Arya, we are glad to see that you are already reaping benefits of this trip and you have learned how to look for lessons in leadership skills in every experience. That is great."

"Yes Bala, thanks to you guys, I am hoping to turn a new leaf once I go back to my work."

Just as we were feeling pangs of hunger, as promised, we could see Pradip driving in and parking his jeep, bringing us some well-deserved homemade dinner. It was filling and hot. We all had dinner on the river bank with moonlight shining brightly over all of us and creating a magic effect on the flowing river.

SUCCESS TIPS :

1. In Life and work, set the bar high and keep striving for better heights all the time.
2. Do not get satisfied with small successes!
3. Let Robots do repeated stuff. Leaders must take calculated risks for rapid growth instead of being content with the status quo.
4. Teams must be taught to make improvements. Try Kaizen all the times.
5. Life rewards little more, to persons who are willing to take little bit more calculated risk!!

TO DO:

1. As a leader, you must lead the Kaizen show. Promote, encourage, monitor and reward Kaizens.

2. Make cross functional teams and set challenging tasks. Help, guide and support the teams.

3. Set Quality, Cost, Delivery and Service targets, at least 1% better than your competitors. Analyse, Explore, Innovate, Metamorphose your teams, their work processes and thought processes.

4. Review all your processes. If you are doing the same thing, without any change or improvement, in the last couple of years, NOW, is the time for change!

5. Gravity is not applicable to Success. Success will not fall in your lap. You have to take risks to go and fetch it!! Do not accept mediocre life.

6. Learn the differences between Rashness, Gambling and Calculated risk.

> Stop Being Afraid Of What Can Go Wrong,
> And Start Being Excited Of What
> Could Go Right
> – *Tony Robbins*

8
CAMEL, HARDWORKING AND TIME MANAGEMENT

After such a physical exertion, we had a wonderful sleep in our tents last night. In the morning, after freshening up and a good bath in the river, we folded up our tents, cleaned up the area, picked up all the waste around, and were ready to leave.

"So, let us get ready for about 7-hour ride, and we shall be reaching our next destination. After a couple of hours of driving, we shall be hitting highways and then ride is expected to take place at pretty fast clip" I said.

As expected, Arya chipped in, "I can foresee, today is going to be another adventure, in another place right."

Jiva said "Yes, you are going to ride an animal which you have never ridden before, in your life, till now."

Arya exclaimed, "my God, I wonder how you guys keep coming with something different every time!"

Thus said, we left the river bank and started our ride. The ride took us along some dense forests, to begin with, and slowly and almost imperceptibly, the canvas gradually changed. The river, which accompanied us for many hours yesterday, was the first thing to disappear from our views. Slowly, the tall trees gave way to much smaller trees and shrubs.

"Time for breakfast" Arya's voiced crackled from behind and in Bluetooth. Knowing Arya well, I know he is one guy who always used to skip breakfast. But now in the past few days, his appetite seems to have improved!

We stopped at a small roadside restaurant, and we were served hot Paratha and Yogurt Raita, which was indeed very tasty. Finishing our breakfast with a cup of Chai, and without wasting much time, we proceeded with our journey.

From quiet not so populous mountain ranges, the roads led us to through thickly populated towns and bypass roads, circumventing a couple of big cities.

"Bala, look at the changes, the trees are no more there, rivers are out of sight, the fresh air is lost as we approach the city. Sad, in the name of modern living, we are neglecting nature" said Arya.

"You are right Arya. Already in the name of development, we have killed many rivers, buried and dusted big lakes to develop dwellings, trees have given way to flyovers and the way we are destroying nature and expanding, already one can see the path of self-destruction, unless our ways are changed", I replied back.

Jiva's voice came in, "The statistics show, even our big glacial fed rivers would soon become seasonal rivers and that would be a great hit to the human race, which, unfortunately humanity is slow to realize and respond. Many city dwellers are either ignorant or don't care about the havoc they are creating and leaving such a horrible habitat, to their children."

Arya said, "Yes, even I read that many rivers that were flowing through my city fifty years back have either become sewerage path or disappeared. Maybe there is an apartment block sitting on that disappeared river right now!"

I said, "anyway guys, let us hope each of one of us realize that we do not own the earth, and we have just borrowed it from nature till we live and hopefully hand it over back to nature, in a better way when we pass away. We spoke about it earlier too. We have after all one earth to live, and hopefully not foolish enough to cut the branch we are sitting on."

Our thoughts were on the systematic destruction of nature, by man, as if it belongs to some enemy rather than our own. It appears man has left his rather obscene mark on everything- Trees, Mountains, Rivers, Oceans, Flora and Fauna. It was an alarming thought to realize, what nature and humanity preserved for millions of years is being destroyed by greed, in just 25 or 30 years. Indeed, man is competent!

There was silence as we rode on further. The temperature was increasing around us. The trees had completely given way to short shrubs, and by around lunchtime, there was desert sand all around, we reached a small town in that desert.

We finally stopped and parked our motorbikes near a Hotel. "Bala, another first, I am seeing desert for the first time!" exclaimed Arya.

I said, "Yes, welcome the desert land, and we are going to experience something different here."

We finished our lunch in that hotel. Jiva quickly finished his lunch, went out, and had a long chat with hotel personnel and some local guys. As we were sipping our sweet cold Lassi, Jiva came back with a smile. "Bala, all set to go. In one hour, we are ready to leave."

Arya said, "Leave again? Oh no, we just reached here after such a long ride!"

"Hey Arya, we are not riding motorbike again today, but get ready for a ride of lifetime" assured Jiva.

"Oh, that is what you guys told me in the morning, bring it on, I am ready!", pat came the reply from Arya.

After checking into the hotel and sleeping for a while, we were ready. I told both friends to pick up things which are required for an overnight stay, including some warm clothes in a bag.

As we came out of the hotel, there was a jeep with four local guys waiting for us to whom we were introduced as Kishan and his team, by hotel personnel.

As the afternoon was growing into the evening, we were driven in the jeep for about an hour and went out of that small town deep into the desert where we could see just sand dunes everywhere.

We could see at a distance a Camel cart, a couple of Camels and some people waiting for us. Once we reached them, we got down from our jeep, placed our overnight bags into the Camel-drawn cart. Kishan said, "Guys, two of you get on to one camel each, and another can ride the camel cart."

A look of astonishment came on to Arya's face. "We are going to ride a Camel?"

"Yes" said Jiva "you hop into one Camel, and Bala may be you too, on to another, while I will ride the cart for some distance."

The Camels kneeled to enable us to climb on to their backs. So, thus began our journey with self and Arya in a Camel each and Jiva, Kishan and his team riding the Camel cart. Both our Camels were tied by ropes to the cart, and cart carried not only people, but also water, stove, tents, and other food items.

Arya was beaming with joy and with sheer excitement said, "Oh my God, this is too good! Riding a Camel in the desert which I never thought I would do, in my wildest dreams. So, we are going to stay in the desert today?"

"Yes," I said, "we are going to ride the Camel for about three hours and then once deep inside the desert, we are going to pitch the tents in the desert and spend overnight there."

"Wow that sounds simply out of the world." A child like enthusiasm was exuding from Arya.

The Camels walked with a confident gait, which once one get used to, was easy to ride on. The Camel which was pulling the cart did it quite effortlessly even though there were people and stuff on that cart.

"Never thought a Camel to be of such a strong animal, and it is huge as compared to what we see in a picture or in the TV!" said Arya.

Sunset was approaching fast, and we could see very few people here and there, and soon they too disappeared, and the whole desert looked very isolated. We could look at some wells in the desert, and Arya shouted, "Look over there, did I see some foxes just now?"

Kishan said, "Yes, you will see quite a lot of animals even though it is a desert. These animals have adapted to desert life, and they come alive mainly after sunset. Just look out and be careful with Snakes and Scorpions."

Sure enough, in the next half hour, we could see small gazelle-like deers, quite a few foxes, and many other small animals.

"I can sense the temperature dropping quite fast now" said Arya.

Jiva said, "Yes the night temperature in the desert is expected to be very cold."

We could see that Arya was enjoying his Camel ride quite a bit, and after some time, I got down and went to the cart, while Jiva rode the Camel.

When our caravan finally reached our campsite, it was two hours past sunset, but there was quite a bit of starlight around us. There were no other artificial lights anywhere to be seen. We could clearly see around even with such dim star light and we were amazed how quickly our eyes get accustomed to such changes.

We helped Kishan and his team to set up four tents, one for each one of us and one for Kishan and team. As we looked around, there were huge sand dunes all around, and our tents were pitched in between two huge dunes. Kishan lit and hung the small lanterns in front of each tent.

Kishan said, "While we prepare some Roti and Potato Sabji for all of us, why don't you take an evening walk and come back? It would be a wonderful experience. Just make sure that you carry a compass, since, once you walk about 200 meters, you would not be able to locate our tents amongst other dunes."

It was an excellent idea, and we set off armed with offline Google maps, compass and torches. The gentle slopes of dunes were quite easy to walk across, and the desert sand was smooth to walk on. There was starlight all around which made our tasks more comfortable and there was no need for a torch to be switched on.

As Kishan said, after a few minutes of walk, we could see dunes all around but not our tents. However, our compass and Google maps came handy to know where we are. As the temperature was dropping down, we decided to wear woollen caps.

"Arya, what do you think about these Camels?" I asked.

"Big animals with a big heart. Never thought they would be so strong! They seem to be working so hard in this desert environment withstanding the cold and the hot weather."

"Yes, of course, they are hardworking and surprisingly, they can be very aggressive too if they choose to be! However, in our office environment, what do you think about working hard?"

"Yes, that applies there too, right? The one who works hardest wins, isn't it?"

Jiva chipped in, "True, hard work is an important aspect, but is that the only one quality required for a leader or a manager to have?"

This question made Arya to think for a while. He was walking thinking silently, as he knew it was a trick question.

The warm clothes we were wearing, was protecting us from the cold weather around. We could hear a fox howling at a distance, but they never pose a danger to, at least, a group of men. A few black Scorpions were seen scurrying away.

"Hard work is an essential thing. Along with that, a leader needs to have qualities such as Empathy, Vision, Management skills, etc." said Arya.

"That is what I was coming to" I said, "The leader should have several qualities to be a successful one. One such quality is hard work. However, if the leader ends up just doing hard work, he may not have either time or energy to focus on the other qualities."

I continued, "No leader can boast that, he works for long hours and that alone makes him a good leader. Inefficient time management and not having faith in deputies and thus not delegating can also make a leader to work for long hours! So a leader must list down skills required to face a certain situation, and if one amongst the list is hard work, then it is ok."

Arya chipped in, "Bala, what you said strikes a chord. I remember quite a few 30-minute meetings which had extended up to 2 hours, and thus I and my team members had to put in extra hours to catch up on other things."

"Yes, a meeting can be a time killer, if not planned properly. Have a proper agenda for a meeting, focus on the points with precision and discuss with 'to do' list, which will save much time."

"Yes Bala, I see the point, my God, we have wasted, at least two to three hours, each day, by allowing discussions to veer off to other subjects in meetings."

Jiva added, "By having long meetings, a leader not only wastes his time but hundreds of working hours of his team. Moreover, I feel it is the same difference between 'being busy and being productive', am I right Bala?"

I said, "Jiva, you hit the nail exactly on the head! You guys would have seen many people, including some leaders, who always show themselves to be very busy, but the important question they and others need to ask is, whether they are being productive! A person can also look busy searching for a document or a file and even conducting long unnecessary meetings! What matters is, whether he completed the micro goal he set himself for the day."

And Jeeva added, "And allowed his teams to complete the tasks set for the day!"

Arya added with a little sheepish smile, "To accept the truth, I looked busy to others, but I know that either I was catching up for my lousy time management, or as you said, searching for some file, paper, or document and thus looking busy."

Just then Jiva said, "Guys watch out, look there" we all looked in the direction he showed. A few feet away from us, a small snake was crawling away, on the sand.

I said, "Jiva, thank God for the starlight and your alertness. Though these snakes avoid humans, it is always better to be cautious. However, generally, they are harmless and would rather run away from us."

Arya was short of breath. "Surprising, where these guys hide in the day time? Good heavens, we just missed getting bitten by one of them!"

I said, " They stay in the cooler confines of underground burrows or under a rock in day time" and added, "Coming back to our discussion, a leader must not only follow time management himself, but make sure his team's time is also not wasted. Identify time wasters and eliminate them to ensure unnecessary bull work is not carried out, to compensate for the time lost."

We realized, we had walked a fair bit of distance and decided to return to our tents.

Jiva said, "It appears there is no need for compass or maps. Our footprints are so clearly visible on sand. We need to just follow them back to our tents". And we started to trace back our steps back to our tents.

Arya said, "Now I realize why my team members were a little bit upset with me as a leader. I realize I kept conducting unscheduled long meetings to keep myself updated on what is happening rather than to find solutions. I also shifted away from the subject many times. I think I have been wasting my team members' time quite a bit. But now, I learned about, not just being busy but learn to be productive, whatever be my level in my organization."

Jiva said, "That also gives more time for you to be with your family which creates a sense of satisfaction."

I added, "Remember. Do not get me wrong. Working hard and with passion, is indeed required for growth. However, one has no right to mess up with the schedule of our team members due to our inefficiencies and insecurities."

Arya was smiling, "Bala, the whole discussion started by an innocuous question from you 'What do you think about these Camels?' and see where we ended up! Indeed you have a way of cleverly guiding the discussion to where you want, right?"

I laughed and said, "No Arya, though I try to nudge the discussion towards learning something, there is a big learning by looking at animals such as Camel and introspect ourselves on our style of working. Isn't it?"

From his backpack, Jiva pulled out cups and a flask with hot tea.

"Wow that is very nice of you! I did not know you were carrying that," I said.

"Kishan thoughtfully gave me this flask, when we started our walk."

Thanking Kishan, we sat on the dunes and keeping an eye on the movement of scorpions or snakes, and enjoyed our sips of tea. Innumerable stars were visible and if one listened carefully, when the wind flowed over the dunes, it created a whistling noise which was melodic. We all enjoyed our tea in silence, each going through the day in our own perspective.

When we reached back to our tents, hot Rotis and Sabji was ready. Three Camels were munching away the grass brought on the cart. All of us sat together and had a wonderful dinner. When we were about to retire, Kishan warned us to make sure that we check the tents with torchlight for the presence of any insects and keep the tent tightly zipped throughout the night.

Though it was very cold and windy outside, each shelter was provided with very thick blankets to keep us warm while we had a nice sleep.

SUCCESS TIPS

1. Meetings must have a pre-declared start time and end time. So follow it!
2. No unplanned discussions on other subjects which are not scheduled.
3. Respect other people's time, you have no right to waste others' time.
4. Introspect on every task and check whether it keeps you busy, or it takes you a step closer to your goal.
5. Keep your workplace neat, tidy and creative. Unkempt work place can, surprisingly, eat away your time very fast.

<u>TO DO</u>:

1. Do not neglect, if someone frequently works long hours. Find out whether it is due to his inefficiency accumulated throughout the day, or he genuinely needs support.

2. Conduct extremely efficient meetings. Circulate agenda, duration of meeting, start time, end time etc. much in advance.

3. Do not use meeting to show off your knowledge. Listen more, give precise decisions. Ban distractions such as mobile calls etc. during a meeting

4. Importantly, you go well prepared to meeting too!!

5. Prepare a chart and capture details as to where and how you spend time. You will be surprised to see, how much time can be saved by eliminating time wasting activities.

6. NEVER ignore your family for your profession. Do you take your family out for dinner, movie, picnic etc.? Or spend adequate quality time with your child? It is not too late. Start at least now!

> Those Who Make The Worst Use Of Their Time, Are The First To Complain Of Its Shortness
>
> – *Jean De La Bruyere*

9
ACCIDENT AND STRESS MANAGEMENT LESSONS

There were dew drops all over our tents when we woke up. It was as if it was raining. We came out of our tents to find the views were magnificent. Sun was about to rise, and there was a yellow light which had began to spread out everywhere.

Kishan and team were already up and preparing some tea. Couple of them were giving a scrub to the Camels which were tied to the carts. Camels were contently chewing the cuds.

Kishan handed over a teacup to each one of us. He said, "Guys, this tea is made with Camel milk, you may please try."

"Tea with camel milk?! But how does it taste?" said Arya.

"Taste would be almost the same as cow's milk, except it is little thicker and has a distinct taste."

We took a sip of the tea, and it indeed was good! It had a quite a strong flavour but certainly tasted awesome.

The sunrise was gorgeous and tall whitish yellow sand dunes created their own shadows which were in proportion to the height of the dunes. The Camels were being taken for a walk to drink water from a nearby water storage point meant for animals and Kishan prepared bread sandwiches for all of us.

He said, "Let us quickly finish our breakfast and move out of this place before the sun gets hot, which happens quite early in these parts."

We packed, helped Kishan and team to pack our tents, the Camels too got ready for the ride back to the town. One Camel was ready to pull a cart, and all our luggage and other stuff were put in that cart. We all sat together and had a good breakfast.

"Kishan, how many days in the month will you have this business of taking tourists out for a desert ride in a caravan, to stay overnight as we did?" I asked.

"Not many days" replied Kishan, "You were one of very few Indian tourists who showed interest in an overnight stay in the desert and for a Camel ride. Somehow many local tourists still play safe and stay in the town. Normally we bring about 7 to 8 groups of foreign tourists for such desert stays every month."

We were just thinking, why not more and more Indian tourists too enjoy such beautiful experience of staying overnight in deserts.

During our journey back to the town, Arya took a Camel cart ride while Jiva and I rode the Camels. Though it was still a very early morning, the Sun was glowering down on us, and our skin was becoming drier with the hot weather. The sand too was, too jarring to look at, since it was reflecting the blazing sun.

Thankfully, Kishan had made an alternate plan for us. The return journey took a different route and lasted till our caravan reached the nearest road which was about an hour away. There we could see a jeep was already waiting for us.

"Now we part ways" said Kishan, "This jeep will drop you in your hotel and we ride the camels to reach our village which is not very far from here."

We thanked Kishan and his team for their hospitality and their efforts and jumped into the jeep. Arya fondly patted the Camels which sniffed at him and bared its teeth in a friendly grin!!

After jeep journey of about an hour, we reached our hotel.

"So Bala, what time, should we get ready to leave here?" asked Jiva.

I said, "We will spend a couple of hours refreshing and resting, since we have quite a distance to travel today."

We went to our respective rooms. Had a nice, hot water bath and took some rest. By close to noon, we were ready to leave.

As we revved up our motorbikes, Arya, who was riding pillion with me, asked, "Bala, I have been riding pillion throughout this road trip. Can I ride motorbike for a change?"

Jiva offered to give his bike to Arya and take pillion seat on my bike. "Arya", I said, "Our last activity is going to be something which needs courage, self-confidence, faith on team members but the experience would be something which cannot be described, and only be experienced"

"Come on, Bala, stop playing with words, what are we going to do?!" asked very curious sounding Arya.

Since Jiva and I had planned the whole trip in advance, Jiva replied, "Have you heard about Scuba diving?"

"Yes" said Arya, "I have seen in TV and in some movies too"

"And that is what we are going to do" I added, "That will add another adventurous page to your life."

"What is Adventure to you both seems to be, as usual, a nightmare for me!! Hey guys, now I realize, you guys have gone bonkers. I don't even know swimming properly, and you guys want to drown me in Titanic depths of ocean?!!"

We both were laughing. I said, "Believe us Arya, that would be a fitting climax to this trip. By now you know that even if we take you, as you say, to Titanic depths, we ensure that you come back alive! And trust us, you will not be killed and you will certainly see another day!!"

"Anyway, while on this whole trip, you guys have always taken care of me but have never given me a choice, do I have one now ?!" joked Arya.

He knew by now that, though our actions may put him in new and possibly risky situations, he was learning to enjoy the same, at least after each experience.

I said, "But next offer is something you cannot refuse and anyway, that will happen only tomorrow. Today we shall ride as long as possible, and take a break in between and our Scuba diving will take place tomorrow."

Thus we left that small desert town and started our final lap of the journey. Since Arya was riding for the first time on this trip, we started slowly, giving him time to get used to riding. Anyway, the road was barren with hardly any traffic around. The road cut through the desert sand and was devoid of any trees.

But after riding for about a couple of hours, slowly desert sand gave way to healthy soil, and small trees started appearing. And we hit the six lane highway soon, and the ride was pretty fast. The terrain now was of evergreen forests all around us and ride was turning out to be a pleasant one.

By late afternoon, we decided to take a break and have our lunch. We stopped by a village and had a quick meal before proceeding further.

"Bala", Arya's voice came through Bluetooth, "Since we are going at a quick clip, will it not be possible to reach the beach for Scuba diving today itself?"

"No" I said, "we have at least another 250 kms to go, and there is no point in hurrying, we will stay overnight somewhere and then proceed tomorrow morning."

Just as Arya was about to say something, we could see ahead a village road cutting across the highway. And since it was evening, after grazing, a shepherd was herding his flock of sheep, to cross the highway.

Whether Arya did not see the herd crossing the road, or his attention was diverted for a moment, is not clear, but he realized that he is going too fast to stop in time, from hitting the herd of sheep.

Since I saw the flock on time, I slowed down to a great extent. Arya was not so prepared to do the same. To avoid ramming into the herd, he changed the direction of the bike at pretty high speed, and that made him skid, and he came down in a heap. The speed with which he fell, caused him and bike, together, to skid quite a long way with screeching sound.

As he came to a stop, we stopped our bike and ran towards him. He was caught between the road and the heavy motorbike. All we prayed was, he should be ok. A crowd, mostly of villagers, also gathered quickly to help us. Though Jiva and I were also in state of shock, we realized that the need of the hour is purposeful action.

I parked the motorbike on the side of the road, and promptly went and assessed the situation. I found, thankfully, none of the hot exhaust metal elements of bike were in contact with Arya. With the help of Jiva and villagers, we quickly lifted the bike off Arya.

Arya was writhing in pain, and his ankle seemed to have taken the brunt of the fall, and noticed the skin on his palm has been scraped away, due to the fall. I asked villagers to quickly to bring some water, using which, I washed his wounds in the palm. I told Arya not to move.

I went to my motorbike and quickly brought the first aid kit. Applied some medicines on his wounds. Then I told him to slowly move his ankle and inspected. A small external injury was visible but there was no swelling, and when I touched his ankle, Arya said there was not much pain.

I sighed with relief. It appeared that the pain in the ankle was due to the sudden weight of the bike falling on it and nothing more serious. And the special riding jackets we were wearing, also avoided injuries to his elbows and shoulders.

Jiva was checking his motorbike, and except for broken indicators and some scratch marks on sides, thankfully, he found no significant damage to the bike. Jiva revved the engine and found it to be ok. All the while, Arya, though was mumbling something out of pain, was generally ok and was keenly observing what we were doing.

It was already late evening. The villagers offered to help us in whatever way they can, and I asked for someplace in their village where we can pitch our tents on, for tonight. They gladly agreed for the same.

We thanked God that it was just a minor accident! We and our motorbikes appeared fit to travel further. A kind soul brought tea for all of us, and we sipped it sitting by the side of the road. I allowed some time for Arya to rest peacefully.

I packed up all the first aid kits, cleaned the motorbike, checked if there was any leak of brake oil or engine oil, etc. The precautionary check indicated everything okay, and Jiva also reported the same on his bike. We found Arya was still keenly and quietly observing us.

A few moments later, a teen aged boy came to us and said, "Sir, I was the one who herded the flock of sheep suddenly on to the road, my apologies. I am sorry." We were moved by his honesty.

I asked him, "What is your name, young boy?"

He said his name was Anil. I said, "Anil, it is so nice of you that, you came and regretted for the mistake you committed. See, nothing serious has happened to any of us and anyway we wanted to take a break from our journey today evening, and you gave us that break!"

Listening to this, the boy brightened and told us he would help us with everything possible by him, during our stay in his village. Anil went to Arya and checked his injuries, and we could see he was feeling guilty.

Jiva told him, "Anil, what you did was not intentional, and now why don't you go put all your sheep in their pen and come back to help us to pitch the tent?" The boy smiled and enthusiastically left.

"So boy, how do you feel now?" I asked Arya. It was almost more than one hour since the accident took place. He said, "It could have been a lot worse than what it is now, right? Anyway, sorry Jiva, for getting your bike damaged."

"It is okay Arya, but now tell us, how exactly did the accident take place? Why could you not slow down after seeing the sheep?" Jiva asked him.

Arya replied, "I am used to another bike, where in the gear shifter, the gears are all down, but in your bike, first gear is down and all other gears are up. When I saw suddenly sheep crossing the road, by instinct I changed gears which made motorbike to go faster rather than slowing down! So the bike simply skidded, when I applied the brake."

We could see Anil coming back, with his grandmother, who was introduced as a local village Doctor!! She inspected Arya, applied some green herbal juice on the palm injury and put a small bandage.

Taking out some oil from a small glass bottle she brought along, she did massage for his ankle, which seemed to produce magic results to Arya. He said after a while that his pain in the ankle was more or less gone.

The villagers identified a small piece of land close to paddy fields, to pitch our tents. Anil helped us to set the tents up and bring Arya's saddle bags from the motorbike. By then, it was quite dark, and villagers left us alone, giving us some rest and privacy. Anil informed us that dinner would be served for us in his home today for which we were thankful to him.

As we sat outside our tents, there were sounds of the bells of cattle which were settling down for the night. Frogs can be heard croaking all around us in the paddy fields. There was also a unique fragrance associated with paddy fields all around us.

Though that village had lights, they were few and far away. There was starlight all around as in the previous night, and we were allowing that beautiful village environment to sink into us.

Arya was looking at us. "I was observing both of you after I met with that accident and I was amazed that both of you worked as if you were trained in the military. There was no panic, no stress, no additional discussion, nothing. You went ahead as if you undertook that drill a hundred times. I was administered first aid, bikes were taken care of, villagers handled nicely. I am sure, I would have panicked in a similar situation."

"Should I take that as a compliment or you are complaining we did not display any emotions towards you after the accident?" Jiva asked him jokingly.

I said, "Arya, it is like this. Any situation involving an unexpected and unfortunate incident would be stressful. There is no point if everybody involved starts stressing around and gets panicked on top of it. Yes, we both are trained in first aid and are experienced in tackling accidental situations like these, as we have faced some ourselves, in some other trips. But if had we got panicked ourselves, believe us, you would have panicked too."

"No doubt" said Arya, "After seeing you both working with intent instead of panicking, actually I was finding myself recuperating better. It is like being patient to a calm Doctor!!"

"Not only here, Arya, even in work, instead of you managing stress, if you allow stress to manage you, the situation can be chaotic. Especially as a leader, one needs to look at the best possible steps in every situation by coming out of the situation and having a look at the situation. That way, not only will you land up with best alternates, but your team also would be confident."

"But how do I do that?" asked, Arya.

"Arya, getting stressed with a situation, does not help you, others and the situation itself. So take a deep breath and take stock of situation. Every few minutes allow the mind to just cool down!! As I said earlier, come out of situation in your mind and think forward. View the whole situation from the perspective of a third person."

This conversation set Arya thinking. He confessed, "Not only for these emergency situations, but there are times, even for small things I get stressed."

I said, "Stress in small quantity is actually good, once a while! But if you feel stressed very often and for very small things, than it is time for kicking out that habit. Remember, stress is very deeply connected to your way of thinking. It is nothing but choice made by you."

"What? Stress is a choice made by me?!!"

"Of course, yes, Arya. How many times you have seen, different people feeling different amount of stress or even no stress, under same so called, 'Stressful Situation'? It is nothing but how you and your mind collude to handle that situation. But you have to remember, lot of Adrenaline gets produced when you are stressed."

"But Adrenaline gets one pumped up, right?" asked Arya

I said, "As I said, a small quantity of Adrenaline, once a while, is ok. But too much of stress results in faster heartbeat, rapid breathing and other side effects, which are quite harmful to your body"

"So I understand that, feeling stressed all the time, is not a good idea at all. Even I am not impressed, when I see some people carry stress around all the time, as a badge of honour!! But how do I manage that?"

Jiva said, "Practice a few things Bala said just a while ago. There are other methods too, which we can discuss once we are back in our city. But along with practice of those things, meditation would go a long way in handling stressful situations in a meaningful way. Instead of feeling stress, you will start considering solutions to the situation! "

"Bala, once I go back to our city" said Arya, "Can you help me to learn meditation?" I assured that I would do so.

At a distance, we could see Anil coming towards us, to take us for dinner.

We joined him and walked to his home for dinner, and half of the village was there to welcome us! They were really curious to know who we are, what we do, and whether we take such motorbike trips often. I narrated some anecdotes from our trip. They eagerly lapped it all up.

The dinner indeed was delicious, to say the least, and they had even prepared special local dessert for us. Shortly after dinner we said good night to Anil and the villagers and returned back to our tents.

"Bala" said Arya, "your handling of situations with humbleness and tact, has won us so many friends, including Anil, who was more or less, the reason for an accident!"

I said, "In any situation, being humble is the hallmark of a truly great human being. As they say, deep water does not make noise. But you need not be subservient to anybody, and remember, arrogance can win a battle, but humbleness and kindness to fellow human beings can win a war."

We decided to call it a day and with Arya informing that grandma's treatment is working well, we entered into our respective tents for a good night's sleep.

SUCCESS TIPS

1. Train the team members well, before they are entrusted with any task.
2. Any change in product, process or a machine needs training and retraining.
3. Learn meditation. It helps you to organize your thought processes.
4. Circumstances, which may be beyond your control, may create situations. But it is your choice to get stressed or not.
5. What is stress for one person can be an action point for another.
6. You will live more happily, if you start forgiving people for their mistakes!
7. The junior most team member may be your biggest ally. Respect everyone.

TO DO

1. Start preparing a "Stress Diary". Note down, each day, what made you to feel stressed, and take counter actions.

2. Keep aside every day, thirty minutes as, "worry time". In that time, think, analyse and understand all your, so called "Worries". You are not going to worry at other times!

3. Most of the time, your stress or worry may be due what had happened in the past, or what will happen in future. Learn but forget the past, plan for the future and enjoy the present.

4. Sleep deprivation is one of the key reasons for stress. Switch off mobile, TV, Laptop etc., at least thirty minutes before bed time. Listen quietly to the sounds of waves, water, birds, wind chimes or instrumental music of your choice, just before bed time.

5. Never try to drown stress with Alcohol, Nicotine or Caffeine. They are temporary suppressants, with sometimes dangerous side effects. Find out and eliminate root cause for stress.

6. NEVER miss your breakfast or other meals, however busy you are.

7. Exercise often. Learn deep breathing (it ups the release of Endorphins, a "Feel Good Chemical") and meditation. The mental, physical, emotional and spiritual benefits of meditation are phenomenal and are scientifically proven.

It Is Not The Load That Breaks You Down, It Is The Way You Carry It

– *Lou Holtz*

10
SCUBA DIVING AND SAFETY CULTURE

The roosters in the village decided we had enough sleep and started crowing to wake us up early in the morning! We felt totally refreshed. Except for the injury in his palm, Arya was feeling he was ready to face the day. The morning was bright, and the rice fields were brimming with early morning sunlight.

A brood of chicken was scratching the ground and preening themselves in front of our tents. The farmers were already up and working in their fields to beat the heat of the late morning. Anil came and wished us good morning and took us to a nearby river, for a bath. After bathing, we returned to our tents and Anil's grandmother had already brought morning breakfast for us.

She beamed towards us and said, "I have prepared local rice pudding for all of you," and she started serving us breakfast with a liberal dose of ghee. While Arya was having his breakfast, she checked the injuries of Arya, and she expressed satisfaction at what she saw.

We felt really thankful to the villagers, Anil, and his grandmother. Expressing our gratitude, we packed our tents and were ready to move on.

The whole village was standing and waved their hands, bidding farewell to us as we started our motorbikes. Arya took pillion seat behind me, and it was almost 9.00am when we began our journey. Though it was a six lane highway, we took care not to ride very fast, keeping yesterday's incident in mind.

But since the roads were excellent, we were fast approaching the beach which was our next and final destination.

"I can smell the sea!" said Jiva, who always enjoyed a swim in the ocean. Yes, of course, we all could smell that typical saline smell of Ocean.

Shortly around lunchtime, we reached the beach town. We checked into a beachside resort. All three of us were served with tender coconuts, as a welcome drink. Arya said, "Wow, the resort is just fantastic. Just look, the beach is just about hundred meters from our room!!"

"Yes indeed, it is not for nothing, this resort is one of the well-known resorts around here" said Jiva and added, "They have their own teams who organize for scuba diving, and I have arranged for today's evening session for us."

"In every location", Arya said with genuine expression of awe, "I am observing that you both have made lot of effort to ensure the things are well organized. I am sure you must have spent a few days, back in our city, arranging for all these things over phone and internet."

We both smiled and just nodded. We spent quite a bit of time before we started our trip, by going through maps, locations and contacting various friends, to make sure that things are ready when we reach each location. But we know that the effort was certainly worth, after seeing the result in all these days, which went without any major glitches.

The rooms were neat and tidy. We gave ourselves a couple of hours to rest and recuperate from our ride. Jiva could not wait any longer, "Can we go for a swim in the ocean?"

I understood his eagerness for a swim. "Sure, but let Arya stay at the shores since the sea is pretty rough."

We changed our dresses and got ready for a swim in the ocean. A person from resort reception called out, "Come back soon since, you will all be undergoing a training session for Scuba in our swimming pool."

We said ok, and Jiva was the first person to jump into the ocean like a fish into the water. I warned Arya, "When the salt water touches your wound in your palm, for some time you will get burning sensation. But believe me, salt water can be the best medicine for your injury!"

And instructing Arya to be in shallow waters near the shore, we both went for a swim.

The water was warm and clean, for a good swim. The swim had a soothing effect on our body, and the waves acted with massaging effect, removing our tiredness in a jiffy! Near the shore, we could see Arya writhing his hand in pain. I told Jiva, "Poor guy, he must have put his injured palm in the ocean water. But I am sure his injuries will heal faster!!"

Jiva laughed and nodded his head in agreement. After a while, literally I had to pull Jiva out of the ocean, and we both swam towards the shore where Arya was waiting in the shallow water for us. "Hmmm, I wish I had learnt swimming. I would have joined you guys."

"Why not Arya? Once we reach back to our town, keep that as one of the point in your bucket list, and we will help you to tick it off so that you can swim confidently in our next trip", I said to Arya who finally gave a smile.

We were taken to the swimming pool inside the resort, and we could see already a team of people waiting for us. They would accompany us until we complete our Scuba diving session. The leader introduced himself. "Hi I am Ajay, your dive master and this is my team. The swimming pool session is to acclimatize you all, to being in the water and making yourselves comfortable."

"By the way" Arya asked, "what is meant by Scuba?"

I said, 'Self Contained Underwater Breathing Apparatus' is the full form of Scuba. It helps one to swim underwater without need to holding your breath. Oxygen is supplied from a tank which you carry on your back. Let's start our training."

Next one hour was spent, with Ajay training us, to make sure we were comfortable in the water and to learn to handle Scuba equipment used while diving. Lessons were imparted on how to use the oxygen cylinders and most importantly how to learn to breathe with the mouth instead of with the nose while wearing the mask underwater. Sometime was also spent on how to clear the water off the mask, while diving, in case if water enters into the mask.

"What an elaborate training!" exclaimed Arya, "I did not know, so much of preparation goes behind each dive."

"Indeed, Arya" Ajay chipped in, "Diving is a dangerous adventure sport, and a lot of preparation and safety measures go into the initial readiness and preparation, before actual dive takes place."

Once we completed our training in the swimming pool and finished a quick light lunch, we were ready to go. A motorboat was waiting for us near the shore. We three, Ajay and his two team members jumped into the boat.

We helped Ajay and his team to load Oxygen cylinders, flippers, swimming suits and other equipments into the boat. We also took drinking water, some snacks, and biscuits along with us. "Why drinking water and snacks for such a short trip?" asked Arya.

Ajay replied, "Arya, we will be travelling in this boat for about an hour, and our diving spot is close to 20 kms from the shore".

We understood that Arya thought we are just going use the boat to go across a few hundreds of meters from the shore!!

Ajay understood the thoughts of Arya. "The diving spot should have water with clear visibility, with some reefs in it and in undisturbed areas. Though there may be fishes everywhere, to sight them properly, we need to go to specific sites. And reefs are some of the best places to see fishes in their natural habitat"

The initial ride across swelling waves near the shore was rough, and once we were past them, the movement of boat became more predictable and smoother. The boat was a medium size one, with a capacity to provide seats for about 20 people. As the motor boat picked up speed, the shore was slowly disappearing.

"I am scoring several firsts in this trip. This is my first boat trip in any ocean. I neither had chances nor courage to take up such a journey in the past. Thank you guys for these adventures."

We just smiled and continued to enjoy vast ocean.

The ocean gave another perspective on our lives. While we have travelled to Moon and Mars, which are tens of thousands or even millions of kilometres away, man is yet to explore many places under the ocean on our own earth!

We have read that the sea makes up 2/3rd of the planet, and that cannot be perceived or seen, if we are on the land. Our thinking that, we are safe on land will change the moment we travel on ocean! It contains innumerable unexplored mysteries, still, with it. It is a world in itself.

"Once we are away from the shore, it appears, there is just the ocean all around with no landmarks," Arya broke his thought and asked, "Just with the compass and with some instruments, it is amazing how these boatmen reach their destinations."

Jiva said, "Some fishermen do not even use a compass, they use their experience and look around to see the stars and ocean currents, to decide the direction and then move on."

Few Seagulls were flying very close to our boat, skimming the water to look for some food.

Much to our disappointment, in spite of moving so many kilometres into the ocean, we could see lot of plastic materials floating on the surface. We could see plastic water bottles, thermocol pieces, used and torn nylon fishing nets, plastic covers, etc.

I said, "Though I am trying to keep quiet on this subject, I am not able to!! We only hope human species soon learns to respect nature, for our own survival. It is a fact, that, we have polluted oceans with millions of tonnes of plastic and micro plastic by our act of using plastic indiscriminately in almost every household items."

Jiva added, "I understand that these microfibers of plastic have already entered into our, animal and fish food chains."

I replied, "Yes, as of now, most of us are consuming fishes and other sea foods, which are infected with micro plastics or with some contaminated chemicals and metals such as Mercury. Scientists predict, maybe, in another 20 years, the weight of plastic in the ocean will exceed the weight of all the fishes put together, which would be a tragedy for the human race."

Jiva and Arya understood that I was very upset.

"Yes, Bala," said Jiva, "We need to use more natural materials and more recyclable plastic rather than single-use plastic and avoid such a disaster which is such a short time away. Tough job to do, with most humans just thinking more about commercial profits and about themselves rather than sustainability of the human race and other species on longer term, on the planet."

I said, "Arya, I do know that at every opportunity, I talk about the environment, about the greediness of humans, but now I hope you understand that Management lessons are just for improvement whereas Environment issues are a matter of survival!"

Thus said we kept quiet and hoped that every single person on this planet realizes what mess we have created in the last fifty years to this beautiful planet and take corrective actions for survival of our own species!!

Mother Earth will, of course survive and prosper without us, as and when our human species might get wiped out, but can we live without Her?!! Should we wait for Her to correct us through Her cruel lessons?!

We watched in silence the hypnotic movement of the boat over the ocean. Arya was silent and was probably allowing sinking in, of the unforgettable experience of travelling in a boat, on a late afternoon, amidst this vast ocean.

The ocean water, which was light brownish when we left the shore, was becoming slowly bluish in colour and shortly the water turned to alluring turquoise blue.

Ajay said, "Can you see a small island over there that is approaching us? We are going to dive around that island in a short while". In about 20 minutes we reached close to that island. Our boat stopped, and the engine was killed.

Ajay and his team very professionally prepared us for the dive. We wore the diving suits which were laden with Lead metal blocks. The oxygen cylinders were checked and rechecked and were mounted on our backs and strapped. We wore swimming jackets which will control our buoyancy.

We removed our sandals and slipped our feet into flippers. And they fixed the face masks to which tubes from oxygen cylinders were connected. We could see Ajay and his team checking and counter-checking each item and processes, many times to ensure absolute safety.

Finally, Ajay said, "Guys, we are ready. Once again reminding you, if you follow safety instructions taught to you during the orientation course and just follow us, it is enough. Each one of you would be accompanied by one of my team members. Since we cannot talk underwater, I would teach you some hand signals which you may use to draw our attention, underwater."

Thus informing, he taught us, few hand signals to be used, as required. He also took out a waterproof picture card, with pictures of various fishes with him. He explained and showed us different types of fishes that we might come across, underwater. We saw Arya was facing some challenges! He was having a little bit of struggle to carry the weight of a cylinder on his back.

I said, "Arya, you will not feel the weight of Oxygen cylinder, once you are in water. Scuba diving is not something you are going to do every day in your life. Just enjoy but follow the safety instructions. And once you are in the water,

Ajay would be with you most of the time, since you do not know swimming. But as you will understand soon, knowing swimming is not a must for Scuba diving, when you are with an experienced instructor."

Finally, we all jumped into the water, and there were few moments of disorientation, and then we could see each other in the crystal clear water. Arya struggled a little bit more, but he was personally guided by Ajay.

Though I and Jiva knew swimming and have done Scuba diving about half a dozen times, for safety reasons, Ajay instructed us to be just around him and anyway, two of his team members were with us, all the time.

The experience of the next 45 minutes was indescribable, and the beauty of seeing shoals of colourful fishes amongst the reefs was unforgettable. There were fishes which were a just few millimetres long, to small hammerhead sharks which were about 5 feet long. The sharks were just curious about us and went off after some time.

We were moving through the shoals of fishes of all colours. They were all within touching distance. Ajay took us around the coral reefs and with the picture card with him, showed us all the types of fishes visible. Amongst the coral reefs, we could even see Moray Eel, a snake-like fish. Ajay advised not to go too close since they can bite pretty badly when approached carelessly.

As we finally started back, a shoal of big electric rays, swam past us, flapping their huge pectoral fins. They were swimming between us and the surface of the water. The moment was magical and mesmerizing.

Slowly we reached the surface of the water and were pulled into the boat one by one. Arya wanted to spend a couple of minutes more inside the water and by using his face mask, he was having one last long look into the ocean before he was pulled in too !

Ajay and his team helped us to remove the cylinder, jackets, etc., and soon we changed to our dry cloths. "I have heard of heaven" Arya said, "But I saw one today! What a fantastic sight we had over there" he pointed at the ocean, still taking in the fantastic views we had, down there.

He continued, "It was simply magic of the nature, seeing so many colourful fishes, in their natural environment, with different sizes of them swimming along with us, in the backdrop of coral reefs and across vast Blue Ocean. Wow! What a great time I am having!" We could understand him, since we were also in similar thoughts.

Ajay said, "Even though I have done hundreds of dives, every time I get into the water, still I see it as a colourful painting done by the expert hand of God. Scuba diving is something, need to be experienced and cannot be explained! So, Arya, it is no wonder, you being first time diver, experiencing such a great pleasure."

We were pretty hungry, and as the boat started its return journey, we shared the snacks and biscuits amongst all of us. Ajay had, thoughtfully, brought tea in a flask and after all that time in the cold water, the hot tea was the next best experience to have!

By the time we reached half-way through our return journey, night had fallen, and our boat was riding over the waves slowly under a starlit sky.

Jiva decided to just lay down and watched the starlit sky, whereas Arya was standing silently near the edge of the boat holding a railing, and was watching the Ocean and the sky intently, taking in the experience. Soon, we could see lights of the shore shortly at a distance, and we touched the beach by 7.30 pm.

We thanked Ajay and his team for their professionalism and for safely bringing us back to the shore. Once they left in their jeep with their equipments, we walked to our resort. A nice dinner was waiting for us. They had prepared dinner with fresh seafood and they served food in a table set just outside the restaurant, facing the ocean.

We could see most of the restaurants had set their tables outside their restaurants allowing clients to enjoy the fresh sea breeze. It was a small town with many tourists pouring in, and we could see all of them were enjoying some good drinks and food. And after dinner, we sat on the beach with sounds of waves breaking, around us.

"What a day I had", Arya repeated what he said on the boat earlier. "We started the day by watching the sunrise amongst paddy fields, rode almost 250 kms, reached here and had a great diving experience which I will remember for this lifetime!"

"Yes", Jiva said, "It was a long day, but certainly we were with Mother Nature most of the time, which is the most refreshing thing."

Except for the sound of wind making rustling noise amongst nearby trees and sounds of waves, it was very quiet. The Ocean is so mighty but still remains calm, at least mostly!

I broke the silence, and said, "Ajay was too good, he really took care of us well. There are hundreds of things that could have gone wrong if he had not checked everything and ensured our safety. There could have been an oxygen leakage, faulty jackets, incorrect face masks, failure to manage the water pressure as we dived down and so many other things."

"Yes, I could see, Ajay took enormous safety precautions to ensure we return back safely" Jiva added, "All our enjoyment and the beautiful experiences we are talking of now, would have turned into a nightmare even if one small thing had gone wrong. Especially with nature, who is merciless if we take Her for granted."

"Initially, I thought swimming pool session was a waste of time" said Arya, "But the even smallest learning in that swimming pool session came in handy when I actually dived into the ocean. And Bala, as you said, I realize that the diving can be very unsafe activity if one does not take safety precautions."

I continued, "Not just Scuba diving alone Arya, even at home, work and everywhere, if you do not follow safety habits, our experiences and enjoyment can turn quickly into sad nightmarish incidents. We think that following safety habits is for the sake of either law enforcing authorities or for superiors, without realizing safety habits must be followed, for our own safety!!"

Jiva said, "May be due to the huge population we have, the respect for human life appears to be little low, as compared to other countries. But now with a more educated population, I see slowly a better trend is emerging with regards to safety habits."

"Yes, there are times in my office, where I pushed my team even at the cost of sacrificing safety habits, just to reach the goals."

I said, "Somebody said, 'when you cut corners, you create more corners'! The most dangerous aspect of by passing safety is, God forbid, should some untoward incident happen, it has the potential to damage the business and reputation of the organization, very badly. Unfortunately many business owners and managers ignore this aspect, until it is too late."

Jiva added, "Not only in office. Even at home or on road, where we are on our own, it becomes even more important that we follow safety discipline"

Arya probed. "Bala, do we need stronger law to ensure people follow safety practices at office, home and on road?"

I laughed. "Yes, to some extent the existing law can be tweaked. But what is more important is each and every individual follows law of the land with their heart and soul and not for sake of law enforcing authorities. After all, those laws are for our own safety!! Isn't it?"

The sea breeze was very calming, and sipping the tea we had brought along, we spent time talking less and thinking more. After spending about an hour on the beach, we decided to return back to the hotel.

"So, tomorrow, we shall be reaching back to our city and will be at home by this time" said Arya.

I said, "Yes, after having enjoyed the break from work and experiences, time to relish the experience and put learning to work too."

The bed was very inviting after such a long day, and I fell asleep the moment I hit the bed.

SUCCESS TIPS

1. Don't hesitate to experiment and experience life in different dimensions.
2. Push the body and mind to learn something new all the time, else you are going to age faster.
3. Nature is the best anti-stress medicine. Walk, trek, swim, or climb.
4. For every activity you undertake, make sure that all safety precautions are in place. Consider safety of others and property around you too.
5. A small careless mishap can cause disproportionate losses in terms of time, pain, money and even your career.
6. Do not ignore the smallest of safety instruction. It is there because somebody else has suffered by ignoring it!

TO DO :

1. When was the last time you learnt any new skill, which is not directly connected to your profession? Music, Painting, Trekking, Blogging – anything will do.

2. Start writing "Journal of Gratitude" every day. There are lot of small beautiful things around, for you to say, "Wow!!"

3. Whatever your position in your organization, learn how to conduct safety audit, list down all Unsafe

actions and Unsafe Conditions and have a plan to eliminate them.

4. Unlike, a motorbike or a car, there are no spare parts available, for our limbs and other parts of the body. So to preserve them, make everybody (both in office and at home) to follow Safety practices.

5. Train your team to log all unsafe incidents too. They are just tip of the iceberg for future accidents.

6. Your teams must know that, you are going to be one big unpleasant guy, if they are found not adhering to safety instructions! Make them realize that, it is for their own good.

> Look Deep Into Nature, And Then You Will Understand Everything Better
> – *Albert Einstein*

11

WHAT IS YOUR POSITION IN YOUR ORGANIZATION?!!

The clatter of Red-wattled Lapwings, which were flying around, making musical noises, was enough to wake us up in the morning. As soon as we woke up, we could hear this mesmerizing sound of waves breaking in the nearby beach.

All three of us gathered on a bench facing the beach. It appeared that there were high tides in the night and we can see watermarks much closer to the resort than we saw in the previous evening. Wondrous are the ways of nature!!

The resort team gave us the option of having either tender coconut water or tea for the morning. I chose tender coconut water while the other two chose tea.

Arya was allowing the scenery around the beach to sink into him. While few people had decided to take a swim in the ocean, some others decided to take a morning stroll in the wet sands of the beach.

Several fishermen, who had gone out to fish in their boats overnight, in the ocean, were returning with their catch, in the morning. The whole beach was buzzing with many activities.

"Our city is about 300 kms from here. What time should we plan to leave here?" asked Arya.

I said, "We will take little easy today. After a swim in the ocean and breakfast, we shall go around this town, which is known for some ancient temples and after lunch in an exceptional restaurant, we will start by around noon. And by the way, how is your palm?"

Arya spread out his palms, and the wounds were almost healed! "As you said, the salt water of the ocean appeared to have done some magic on my injuries. No pain too!"

"Glad to hear that, Arya" said Jiva and added, "Bala, shall we go out for a quick swim in the ocean?" Knowing his eagerness for a swim, I smiled and nodded.

All of us spent the next hour in the ocean water swimming, and Arya was seen to be more confident with the ocean and found trying out his swimming skills in shallow water!!

The buffet breakfast had a good spread of Indian and continental recipes, and after breakfast, we went out to explore the town. There were several ancient temples including one near the shore itself.

We could not but help wondering about the extremely high skill levels of the architects, masons of those structures who constructed such magnificent temples more than a thousand years back.

"Imagine the passion, dedication and hard work put in by those people then, that too without any modern construction equipment, tools, etc." said Arya admiring the temples and those great people of the past. He also bought some memorabilia in some shops selling goods made of seashells.

By noon, we reached a restaurant run by a French gentleman who had married a local girl. He decided to open a restaurant after his marriage and had settled down here with his wife.

"Arya, I know you love seafood and look no further than this place for a fabulous treat." The menu was quite vast, and we chose our stuff and were told our orders would be ready in thirty minutes. Meanwhile, we were served lemon juice. The restaurant had an old world charm and was built with red bricks.

Deep in thought, Arya said, sipping his juice, "So friends, we would be reaching our homes by tonight. And Bala and Jiva, I must thank both of you for taking such good care of me and guiding me through each day, keeping in mind that this is my first motorbike trip."

"Our pleasure, Arya" I said, "Myself and Jiva have gone on quite many trips together, but it was nice to have you with us, this time. I hope, you enjoyed our company and liked the experience."

"Guys, it is not just being with you, which was good of course, but almost every day, I had a learning session through our experiences on our trip. It was almost like a Business Class on Wheels! When I really sit down and think, the trip also played the role of a training program for me. I did not realize that there are lessons to be learnt everywhere. You trained me to see those lessons around us during this trip. I am glad I made time to join you guys."

He continued, "But, one thing I noticed was, though I was a novice in road trip and though I gave troubles to you, I never noticed you getting worked up. You never showed even a hint of impatience with my ignorance and lack of experience or express disappointment with me. How did you manage that?!"

I said, "Arya, there is a wonderful word in English. It is called Empathy. Believe me, it is a very significant word. Simply put, it means, you think in the perspective of the person in front of you. So when the other person makes mistakes out of inexperience, ignorance, etc., instead of just getting angry or showing disappointment on another person, put yourself in his shoes, analyse why he committed that mistake."

I continued, "Maybe that mistake was not intentional. Maybe you also would have made that same mistake, in his place. Once, you learn to think in that way, you start seeing things in solution based perspective rather than a problem finding perspective. After all, we also have made several mistakes in the past during our first few trips."

Jiva added, "You see, it is easy to be tough on people who are junior to us. For example, shouting at our small children or physically weaker people. One knows, in all possibility, they are too timid or afraid to shout back. But, being in a leadership position, we are put on a more responsible pedestal. Shouting at our juniors is not the tool that needs to be used at every opportunity."

He continued, "Our teams look up towards us and what they need is processes for success, demonstrating the process and accepting their initial mistakes and guiding them to eliminate the mistakes. The position power is transient and not long lasting, but leadership power achieved through a cheerful team working for you, and this power is a long lasting one and a satisfying one. We touched on this subject earlier too."

"That was superb, I know Bala can give his thoughts clearly, and nice to see Jiva too put his thoughts in a condensed way" said Arya, "Thinking of my office, yes, I think I was too carried away by my positional power and tried to dominate my team rather than strengthening their hands towards a common goal."

"In this road trip, you have made quite a good number of confessions!" I said.

I added, "It is also important to realize that many a times, we reach positions of power, not only because of just our hard work or skills, but also due to the situation, legacy, a Godfather, and sometimes due to pure luck and coincidence. So let us not take that positional power too seriously."

The lunch was served with a good spread of seafood. I must say that, thanks to the proximity of the Ocean and the personal supervision of the restaurant owner, the quality of the seafood was superb. The French owner of the restaurant came in person to our table, sat with us. We shared some of our past few days' experiences with him, and he said, maybe, in our next bike trip, he might join us too.

Once we were back in our rooms after our lunch, we packed our things for one last time and strapped the saddle bags to our motorbikes. Checked vital signs of the bikes and were ready to go. Arya took pillion seat of my bike.

Surprisingly, though, we had covered more than 3500 kms during this trip, none of us were, that noticeably tired! Maybe we were not noticing our tiredness due to the adrenaline pumping through us throughout our trip.

It was around 1.00 pm when we finally left that beautiful beach town, and the sun was shining down on us. We started rather slowly sinking in the sight of the ocean which can be seen on one side of the road for quite some time. We wanted to capture every moment until it lasted! We live in a city where the ocean is a far off stuff and thus took in the views gladly.

After about 30 minutes of the ride, we and our machines warmed up, and the road was slipping past us pretty fast.

Both Arya and Jiva were silent, and I can understand that many thoughts are going through their mind. Arya, for sure, seems to be quietly going through experiences he acquired in the past few days. During the trip, I noticed that he was writing a diary on every single day, I found him writing quite elaborately in that diary.

I was hoping he really enjoyed the trip. It was nice to see Arya, keeping his mind open to learning something new every day. And from what I observed and what he expressed, I understood he picked up critical lessons which would come very handy when he goes back to the office.

I was also glad that Jiva and I were able to transform a person for better and was happy that he saw himself and understood the serious damage we are heaping on our environment and hoped he will be someone, who would be a torch bearer in the environment issues.

Slowly the beaches gave way to forests, and forests gave way to villages, and as the small towns started to disappear and gradually the residential, commercial, corporate office buildings began to appear, we could sense we are nearing our traffic-choked city. We thought we will take a break for tea.

It was almost late evening. "Now this is quite a paradox" said Arya with a smile. He had long forgotten his habit of getting frustrated easily, thanks to our trip! "We covered close to 300 kms in four hours, and the last 15 kms is going to take about an hour now, what with bumper to bumper traffic just ready for us!!"

Jiva chuckled, "Welcome back to our city, Arya!"

I said, "As we discussed before, we dwell in our city by our choice, so there is no point in getting too upset about seven million citizens of the city creating some mess!!"

After having the tea, the not so good quality of which, truly reflected we are reaching a commercial hub, we started on the final lap of our journey, which proved to be the toughest one!! With starts and stops and huffs and puffs, we finally reached the coffee shop where, about ten days back, we made our initial plan for our trip. Switching off the ignition, we went inside and ordered for some snacks.

"Arya, I noticed you made a lot of notes on your diary during our trip. Will they be put to use?!" I asked.

Arya smiled, “Oh, you noticed that?! Yes, I did jot down the experiences, the lessons I learned each day and the action plans, which I am confident of putting to use starting tomorrow”.

Snacks were served. “Remember to give adequate time to your family and friends too, for which your wife would be ever thankful to you” said Jiva.

“Wish you all the best both in personal and professional life, Arya. Hope to see you again in our next road trip” I said and bid farewell to him. He booked a taxi to reach home.

I could see many motorists whizzing past us and in total contrast to the past ten days of our experience, there was buzz all around, with drivers honking impatiently, and we could also smell the exhaust fumes of millions of vehicles plying all around us. Without us even realizing, we were longing for those quiet moments amongst rivers, mountains and beaches!!

Jiva and I spent some time chatting, and finally, we took leave of each other and headed to our respective homes.

And of course, though it was a clear sky, the stars which were beaming down on us during our trip during the past few days, were nowhere to be seen!

SUCCESS TIPS

1. Avoid harsh words as they can cause permanent damage in relationships.
2. Before finding fault with others, take a split second time, and think whether you have never ever committed similar mistake yourself?!?
3. Holding anger in you is like holding hot iron in your hand. You will hurt yourself
4. Before showering scorn at your team, view the situation with empathy.
5. Thank God that you are a leader now. Think carefully, 100% of the credit for reaching that position, may not belong to you alone.

TO DO:

1. Your temper is precious, so do not lose it often!

2. Think carefully whether you are abusing your positional power. Stop if you are doing so. One symptom is, you think everyone in the organization is at your beck and call!

3. Good leader is seen in organization, when he is on leave or travelling!! If things move smoothly in the organization, in spite of his absence, then you have created good leaders down the line. A good leader creates more leaders within his team.

4. Listen. In meetings, keep aside your view point, see and listen to things in others' perspective and then come to a conclusion. Remember, empathy plays a core role in Emotion Quotient, EQ.

> Leadership Is About Empathy. It Is About Having The Ability To Relate To And Connect With People For The Purpose Of Inspiring And Empowering Their Lives
>
> – *Oprah Winfrey*

EPILOGUE

It was almost three months since we went on that road trip. Through I was in touch with Jiva couple of times, I could not speak to Arya, after we came back from our trip. My consulting assignments took me out of a country a couple of times, and I had to travel extensively within the country on several projects.

One Saturday morning, as I was sipping my morning tea, my mobile rang. It was Arya. With a smile, I picked up the call.

"Hi Bala," Arya's voice was as chirpy as the Red Wattled Lapwings we heard during our trip!

"Can I drop by at your home? Can you ask Jiva to join too? I will be reaching your place in about two hour time."

It was clear that he was not asking permission but rather informing me that he is coming to my home!! His enthusiasm excited me to know what is up with him and coincidentally I had taken a day off that day, so I asked him to come over to my home soon. Meanwhile, called Jiva and invited him to join in too.

I prepared some sandwiches and fruit juice for them, while waiting. My mind travelled back to our trip. I realized, though I had gone on some road trips earlier, this trip offered a lot of different experiences and a lot of takeaways. Such learning, I found, was helpful and useful in my consulting assignments too.

My thoughts were interrupted by the doorbell, I opened the door to see a cheerful looking Arya standing with a smile and a box of pastries. I welcomed him into my home, offered him some green tea to start with and told him to take his seat.

There was a spring in his walk which exuded confidence in every action.

"So," I started, "Where did you disappear for so many days, Arya? There was no communication at all from your end!"

Just as he was about to answer, Jiva too dropped in, and we settled down for a chat.

"Bala," said Arya, "I was busy totally removing cobwebs from my mind and reconstructing my thought process and prepared a roadmap for the past few months both in my work as well as in my home."

"So, how was the result?" asked Jiva.

"Stunning" said Arya, in a single word. We looked at each other and smiled. I was eager to get more details from him.

"Guys, I know there is a saying in our village which loosely translates to 'Theory can only take you some distance, but the experience is what gets you to complete the journey."

He continued, "Though I have read many books and completed my studies in a Business school, what we all underwent together during that road trip just transformed me. And Bala, I don't know how much to appreciate you for your efforts in discussing and pushing me every day, to learn lessons from our experiences. Those practical tips, and ideas we deliberated upon, during our trip, went a long way in providing me with solutions both in my office and in my home."

I told him, "Thank you Arya, but don't forget the role played by Jiva too. By the way, what do your team members say, now?"

Arya said, "The same guys who were looking at me with fear and loathing, are working like a self-guided missiles. All I did was fine-tune my communication, and use Empathy. I honestly try to understand their problems and suggest ideas. They look at me with admiration rather than as an intimidating boss. I am no more a boss, but a leader" proclaimed Arya with pride.

"That is wonderful Arya!" I exclaimed.

"Do you and your team still work late every day?" asked Jiva.

"No. Not anymore, Jiva" said, Arya, "We have learned to map the time chart now and realized that there were too many time guzzlers, and by eliminating most of them, we now get back home on time. But of course, when a new project is introduced or during a client visit, there are occasions when we stay back, but at least it is not due to inefficient use of our available time."

I served both of them with bread sandwiches and fruit juice.

Sipping mine, I asked him, "I am sure your wife is happy with you now."

"She is, Bala." said Arya "She said after the trip I have gotten better in taking care of her and our kid. I consciously make an effort to give her and our son, undivided attention when I am at home. Seeing that they no longer feel ignored makes me happy myself. We often go out for movies and dinners now. She was right all along. It really feels rejuvenating being with her and have heartfelt conversations about everything happening in our lives on the weekends"

I replied, "Arya, that sounds great and keep going the same way."

Arya thanked me and resumed. "Oh and very importantly, I got the review reports, of those quarterly reviews done yesterday with my bosses, shall we say my business leaders!! They said there has been a big evolution in the way I worked and I seem to be contributing a lot to the organization now. They said they are happy that I had put in the effort to correct all the challenges they pointed out in our previous quarterly meeting."

He continued, "They said, I have become a competent team player, and there is a very positive feedback about me from my team in our 360-degree feedback exercise. And our clients are happy that I have taken up the issues boldly and solving every challenge thrown at me, by them. My management team is pleased that the safety record has improved too, along with other performance metrics."

I did not want to stop his energetic feedbacks coming through and allowed him to complete his sentences! I was really happy about the change in Arya. I still remember, the day I met him at the coffee shop with his bag of disappointments in himself and everyone else before we took on that fun trip! It filled me with joy to see him being revived with self-esteem and confidence.

Arya kept going on, "Dude, I joined Meditation and Swimming lessons too. I wanted to consult you both, but I jumped in before I changed my mind."

Jiva replied, "So, you make time for yourself as well, thanks to your better time management now! That is great!! So, what did you bring in your pastry box?"

"I brought some cake for all us to cut and celebrate my birth in a new avatar!"

We thanked him for the awesome gesture, and I brought a knife from my kitchen. I was delighted and happy to see that Arya could transform himself during that road trip and became a successful leader in his office and a good husband at home.

We laughed and celebrated his rebirth in all its joyfulness, while we cut the cake. As we were celebrating, time moved on and amidst some more of catching up, the afternoon rolled into a joyful night!

FURTHER READING

Chapter 1 : S J Scott. *S.M.A.R.T. Goals Made Simple: 10 Steps to Master Your Personal And Career Goals,* Createspace Independent Publications, 2014

Eliyahu M Goldratt. *The Goal,* Productivity and Quality Publishing Pvt Ltd, 2013

Chapter 2 : Robin Sharma. *5 am Club*, Jaico Publishing house, 2018.

Chapter 3 : Dale Carnegie. *How to win friends and influence people,* Rupa Publications, 2016

Anne Baber and Lynne Waymon. *Make your contacts count: Networking knowhow for Business and Career success,* AMACOM, American Management Association, 2007

Chapter 4 : Yuval Noah Harari. 21 *Lessons for the 21st Century,* Jonathan Cape, UK, 2018

George Ilion, *Top Visionaries Who Changed the World*, Jaico Publishing House, 2018

Chapter 5 : Russ Crosson. *What makes a Leader Great*, Harvest House Publishers, USA, 2014

Simon Sinek. *Leaders Eat Last,* Penguin, UK, 2017

Chapter 6 : Robin Sharma. *The Monk who sold his Ferrari,* Jaico Publishing House, 2003

Gaur Gopal Das. *Life's Amazing Secrets : How to find Balance and Purpose in Your Life,* Penguin Ananda, 2018

<u>Chapter 7</u> : Imai, Masaki. *Gemba Kaizen : A Common Sense Approach to Continuous Improvement Strategy,* McGraw-Hill Education, 2013

Sir Richard Branson. *Screw It, Let's Do It: Lessons in Life,* RHUK, 2008

Anthony Robbins. *Awaken the Giant Within,* Pocket Books, UK, 2001

<u>Chapter 8</u> : Roberta Roesch. *Time Management for Busy People,* Tata McGraw-Hill, 2005

An Article by Forbes Agency Council. *Want to Work Smarter, Not Harder? Follow these following 14 steps. www.Forbes.com, January 2018*

<u>Chapter 9</u> : A Johns Hopkins Hospital's article. *Forgiveness: Your Health Depends on It,* www.hopkinsmedicine.org/health

Allen Elkins. *Stress Management for Dummies*, John Wiley & Sons, USA, 2013.

<u>Chapter 10</u> : Bear Grylls. *Mud, Sweat and Tears.* Published by RHUK, 2012

Basudev Panda. *Industrial Safety, Health Environment and Security,* Laxmi Publications, 2013

<u>Chapter 11</u> : John DeMarco. *Desensitizing Anger: A Comprehensive Anger Management Guide,* Page Publishing, Inc., 2015

ABOUT THE AUTHOR

Dr. A. Balamurugan - Author, Motivational Speaker, Business and People Transformation Coach

Balamurugan, who is debuting with this book, is Director of his Business coaching company, Straightegic Solutions Pvt Ltd. He is a Mechanical Engineer from Bangalore and has an MBA in International Business. Before starting his company, he has been working in senior management levels in various organizations, for close to 30 years.

He focuses on creating and coaching excellence in Business and People in organization. Having practiced creating and running of World class organizations, now he consults and trains organizations on world class manufacturing and modern manufacturing practices. He believes, whatever the investment done by the organization in terms of capital assets, unless employees are loyal, energetic and passionate, the organization cannot succeed. He trains employees and leaders, to convert them into supercharged teams. He has clients in India and abroad.

Well-travelled, he is an avid reader, like to try any adventure sport available! Other than coaching Business Excellence and World class manufacturing, he spends his free time in listening to music, keeping himself fit and playing chess. Dreams of being a big change maker in the way how management lessons are being imparted.

He lives in Bangalore with his wife and son.

He can be contacted through:

✉ bala.a@straightegicsolutions.com

balamurugan1232000@yahoo.co.in

in www.linkedin.com/in/balamuruganbusinessexcellence

Printed in Great Britain
by Amazon

51902736R00099